Networks and Image Handling

THE INSTITUTE OF
PHYSICAL SCIENCES
IN MEDICINE

Networks and Image Handling

Edited by
P S Tofts and R W Cranage

Report No. 52

Published by the Institute of Physical Sciences in Medicine,
2 Low Ousegate, York YO1 1QU, England

In September 1982, the Hospital Physicists' Association (HPA) formed the Institute of Physical Sciences in Medicine (IPSM) as a Company limited by guarantee. The Institute, which was granted Charitable Status in April 1984, was established to promote for public benefit the advancement of physics and allied physical sciences applied to medicine and biology, and to advance public education in this field. For these purposes it was decided, among other things, to transfer the publications activities of the Association to the Institute as from 1st January, 1985. From that date, therefore, all books and booklets have been published by the Institute of Physical Sciences in Medicine.

Printed by Bocardo Press Limited, Oxford

CONTENTS

INTRODUCTION

This report is based on the papers delivered at the 15th Annual Computer Conference organised by the Computer Topic Group of the Institute of Physical Sciences in Medicine. The conference, on 'Networks and Image Handling', was held at the University of Wales Institute of Science and Technology (UWIST) in Cardiff on the 3rd and 4th of July 1986.

'No Computer is an Island', to paraphrase the famous statement about mankind. It is becoming increasingly clear that computers, like people, need to relate to others of their kind in order to function to their full potential, and this is the subject of Part 1 of this report. Modern multi-slice high-resolution medical images typically contain 1000 times the amount of data in the 64 x 64 gamma camera images of a decade ago. Computers have improved in speed and memory size to keep up with this, with a reduction in costs. Systems are now more 'user-friendly', with the emphasis on software that conforms to the user's requirements rather than vice-versa. This continuing improvement in equipment means that things that we thought impossible last year can be contemplated this year and (sometimes) achieved next year. This remarkable growth shows signs of continuing in the next few years, with doubling times of 1–2 years for speed and memory size per unit cost. The second part of this report gives an insight into state-of-the-art methods of medical image handling; some of these will become commonplace over the next few years.

A total of 16 papers were delivered to the meeting, of which 15 are presented here in full and one in abstract form. The two discussion sessions at the meeting have been summarised briefly. An extra paper, 'An overview of image processing in medicine' (not presented at the conference), has been contributed by A Todd-Pokropek; this provides a perspective for many of the subjects discussed at the conference. Although the range of subjects presented was very wide we hope that the papers are written in an accessible way, so that readers will be able to gather useful information and ideas from outside of their own particular field of knowledge. For the first time this report contains an index, which we hope will be of assistance in finding one's way around the material contained herein. This report has been edited and prepared for publication on behalf of the Computer Topic Group of the IPSM.

Finally we are grateful to Link Systems for sponsorship of the colour illustrations on the cover.

Editors:

Dr Paul S Tofts DPhil,
Lecturer in Medical Physics,
University Department of Clinical Neurology,
Institute of Neurology,
Queen Square,
London
WC1N 3BG

Dr R W Cranage DPhil,
Principal Physicist,
Medical Physics Department,
Musgrove Park Hospital,
Taunton,
Somerset
TA1 5DA

CHAPTER 1

Computer Networks at UWIST

H Beedie and D Jennings
Department of Computing, University of Wales Institute of Science and Technology

1.1 Introduction

We consider a computer network as an environment in which a number of machines (computers, terminals, data loggers, filestores, switches etc) can communicate using a set of defined mechanisms. We also outline current network usage and facilities and discuss the implementation and development of UWIST network as an illustration. The institution has benefitted from installing networks widely by keeping open hardware options so that the best cost/performance can be obtained. We have limited ourselves substantially to a single supplier owing to the cost of supporting locally an excessive range of equipment type, but the national and international connections have rendered this restriction unimportant. Primary difficulties have been the expenditure of staff effort (10–15 person years, but this has been repaid by both grant and commercial income), and the indirect benefits of better hardware partly due to acquired expertise. For networks to realise their major benefits and to achieve any stability, communication is governed by tight standards. Whilst these may retard implementation of 'good ideas' they impose a discipline needed in a complex field.

1.2 The ISO network model

The International Standards Organisation (ISO) developed a model for the definition of network protocols in the late 1970s. Their approach was to propose a number of layers defining different levels of service. By strictly adhering to a layered structure it is possible to modify the details of the operation of one layer without in any way affecting the operation of others. The approach therefore allows networks technology to evolve without the need for wholesale replacement of communication systems.

The model is considered as a set of protocols and interfaces. The protocols define the mechanisms for communication between components which are able to set up a virtual communication mechanism. The interfaces define the service primitives of a particular level of the model.

The layers of the model are shown in *figure 1.1*. Briefly their functions are as follows

1. The physical layer defines electrical characteristics of the communications medium.
2. The link layer transforms the transmission medium characteristics into an error free service. Data is broken into frames that may be recognised and synchronised by the link layer processes. The layer is also responsible for handling flow control.
3. The network layer controls a subnet's functions and ensures that data messages are received in the correct order.

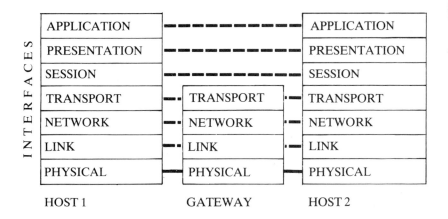

Figure 1.1 Protocols and ISO seven layer model. Solid lines denote physical communications; broken lines denote virtual communications.

4. The transport layer is responsible for end-to-end communication between network processes. The transport layer enables communication across subnetwork boundaries. Gateways can be implemented at this level to enable communication between different address domains or network types.
5. The session layer provides virtual connections between processes so that they may communicate.
6. The presentation layer provides the facilities required to format and compress data, and if necessary undertake data encryption.
7. Application level services are functions provided directly to enable user work. They comprise tasks such as file access and transfer, terminal connection, mail exchange and job transfer.

1.3 Low level protocols

1.3.1 X25

The X25 protocols were originally defined by the CCITT in advance of the definition of the ISO model, but correspond roughly with its first three levels. The Comité Consultatif International Telegraphique et Telephonique (CCITT) is an international body that makes technical recommendations about telephone, telegraph and data communication interfaces. They define communication via serial lines and are typically used at speeds of up to 10 kbit s^{-1}. The protocols define communication in a packet switched network, in which messages are broken into fixed length packets for transmission across the network. The error correction polynomial used by X25 results in an error rate of about 1 in 10^{12}. Some suppliers are now making available X25 products having bandwidths of about 2 Mbits s^{-1}, although the benefits of high bandwidth circuits are not likely to be realised until computer interfaces for X25 networks carry out sufficient of the protocol functions to avoid imposing an excessive load on the host machines. X25 software is available on a wide variety of computers, and there is a good range of suppliers of supporting services.

1.3.2 Ethernet

Ethernet was developed in the early 1970s by the Xerox Corporation, and has subsequently been taken up by other manufacturers. However there has been a simultaneous proliferation in the number of different standards for its use, so it may not be used so readily as X25 in an open environment. Nevertheless progress is being made in this area, and it is likely that by 1988 real open networks will be able to be built using this technology.

Ethernet uses a coaxial cable as a transmission medium, to which all hosts connect. A machine wishing to communicate with another waits until the transmission medium is free, and then broadcasts its messages on the ether. Should another host simultaneously start to broadcast, both hosts detect the colliding transmissions, cease to broadcast, and then wait for a randomly chosen time before attempting to transmit again. The modulation rate of Ethernet is 10 Mbit s^{-1}.

The data rate may vary from 0.5 to about 5 Mbit s^{-1}, although it depends on the length of messages sent across the network. An Ethernet segment may be up to 500 m in length, so Ethernet is typically restricted to operate within a building.

1.3.3 Slotted ring

Standards exist for 'slotted ring' technology in the UK which have been submitted for approval by ISO. The Cambridge Ring uses two twisted pairs modulated at 10 Mbit s^{-1}, and is able in principle to exchange data between any pair of stations at about 1 Mbit s^{-1}. The total data throughput around the ring, between all pairs of stations, can be about 3 Mbit s^{-1}. A station wishing to transmit data waits for a free slot to pass by; this is obtained by the transmitter, marked full, and addresses and data are written in. The receiver marks the slot as having been read, but it is not freed until it has returned to the transmitter. The transmitter may not re-use a slot it has just freed immediately, so reducing the risk of one party saturating the network with traffic. Data is converted from serial to parallel by means of nodes on the ring which converse with host interfaces.

1.3.4 Token ring

There is a standard for token passing rings which is increasing in popularity due to IBM's involvement in the field. In this network type, a token is passed around a ring to each station in turn. When a station receives the token it is allowed to transmit a packet to the ring. When it ceases transmission, the token is passed round to the next station which may then transmit. This continual handing on of the token ensures that no station may saturate the ring with traffic.

1.3.5 Broadband

This is an area where there are few applicable standards. This form of network operates in much the same way as radio transmission where many different channels are frequency and/or time division multiplexed onto one transmission medium. The interfaces are expensive and the networks are inflexible and difficult to install, although very high bandwidths are available.

1.4 Higher level protocols

1.4.1 ISO

Much progress has been made within the last couple of years in formulating these internationally agreed standards. Notably the session protocol is approaching the final stages of agreement, and the file transfer application is stabilising. Within the next five years products to support file transfer, mail, job transfer and terminal access will become available from a variety of sources.

1.4.2 Coloured books

At present the UK academic community has standardised on the use of 'Coloured Book' protocols. These are available for most of the major machine ranges and operating systems used by central services. The use of these products has extended outside the community, including many sites overseas. The services provided cover approximately the same functions as the ISO applications; their use is expected to reduce over the next few years as the protocols are progressively replaced by their ISO counterparts.

1.5 Development of the UWIST computer networks

1.5.1 1978

UWIST was involved in the South West Universities Computer Network (SWUCN) which was a network of ICL machines connected together using software developed in the area. The machines were running a network operating system hich provided many useful features for the submission and control of tasks to be run on remote computers (TASKING). The current Red Book standards were strongly influenced by this product. A Modular One computer, connected to one of the ICL computers, was used to submit jobs to a more powerful CDC computer at the University of London Computing Centre.

1.5.2 1980

UWIST purchased two Digital Equipment (DEC) VAX 11/780 computers and began servicing much more of UWIST's computing requirements locally. These VAX computers were connected by a DECNET link, and also to the British Telecom Packet Switching Service (PSS) network. At this time development was started on the Coloured Book software products in order to transmit files between different manufacturers' computers, initially using PSS as a carrier. The DECNET link only allowed for connections between DEC computers and was found to be expensive in computer resources.

1.5.3 1983

A Packet Switching Exchange (PSE) was purchased to connect the existing VAX computers together using X25. Another VAX (11/750) was also purchased and the PSS link was moved to the PSE. This was the start of the rapid increase in UWIST's local computer networks.

1.5.4 1984

In order to service an increasing number of users' requests for connection to the main service computers, a number of Camtec X25 Packet Assembler/ Disassemblers (PADs) were purchased. These connected up to 16 asynchronous terminals to the PSE and thence to any of the UWIST computers. After initial teething problems with software in both PADs and computers the advantages in flexibility were soon appreciated.

1.5.5 1985

The first of UWIST's high speed Local Area Networks (LANs) was introduced during the summer in the Aberconway building. This was a Cambridge Ring and made use of about 20 RingPADs from Camtec, giving a total of 360 terminal or printer connections. At the same time a number of DEC MicroVAX II computers was purchased, three of these being connected to this network. The Cambridge Ring was connected to the existing X25 network by a gateway thus enabling all terminal users in this building to connect to all of the existing services. There were again teething problems associated with this network, although it must be noted that these problems were not associated with the Cambridge Ring protocols but with higher level software running in the PADs. Most of these have now been cleared up.

1.5.6   1986/7

We are installing another Cambridge Ring in the Bute building and also planning to introduce a third Ring in the last major building. We expect to have about 15–20 MicroVAX II computers connected to the UWIST networks and a total of about 50 PADs. Within the space of about two years, UWIST's computing service will thus have grown from about 150 to about 700 terminal connections. The increase in concurrent terminal users that may be served by UWIST's computers will have also increased by this ratio.

1.6   Network choices

The Computer Board for Universities and Research Councils in the UK advised the use of manufacturer-independent protocols for networks wherever possible, and UWIST followed this advice in 1978. This was a major factor in our decision to implement Coloured Book protocols on the VAX/VMS operating system and also led directly to our purchase of an X25 network. At the stage when we needed a high speed network to connect together an increasing number of computers and terminals, the Cambridge Ring was the only standard which we considered to be well defined and which had available products. A high speed network was thought to be necessary for two main reasons. Firstly, it allowed use of the newer breed of multi-user microcomputers (in our case — MicroVAX II), which give an improved cost performance ratio over larger computers. Secondly, it greatly eased the installation of new terminal wiring and subsequent additional wiring. The cost of the network form of connection for terminals was about the same as for the old direct method of connection to a computer, but the network has obvious advantages in flexibility and ease of expansion. It could be argued that X25 PADs would have been sufficient for our needs, but this would not have followed our philosophy of distributing computer power to where it was needed, and would not have allowed the use of the newer breed of MicroVAX with a limited filestore. We intend to develop software to use the network to move files rapidly between computers thus alleviating the problems associated with this limited filestore.

We also became involved in the development of the software for the network interfaces for our VAX computers. Ethernet was ruled out due to the uncertainty over which of the low level standards would survive, and also due to worries about its stability under conditions of high load. There were no available products for our computers to use the Token Ring, which made the decision in favour of the Cambridge Ring inevitable.

The major disadvantage of the Cambridge Ring is that it is never likely to become widely accepted internationally. This again is not very important. We can use existing high speed gateway products between the Ring and X25 to connect to a widely recognised standard and thence to any new network that we may decide to use in the future.

Theoretical arguments about poor reliability of a network where each of the nodes are active and also where there is one controlling station for the ring structure are spurious. What matters is the reliability of the whole system in practice. We have had no problems with the underlying Cambridge Ring hardware which has performed very well. The problems that we have seen have all been concerned with higher level software running in the PADs and Gateways, which is independent of the form of network.

1.7 Network management

In a network of this size, one of the major problems is managing the many PADs and computers scattered around the site. Monitoring of the systems can however be easily carried out from a central location and to a certain extent, systems may be remotely reconfigured. When setting up such a network, careful thought must be given to the ways in which PADs may be configured, how users are authorised on various machines, and how connections to the outside world, together with their associated costs, are managed. We have developed some software for the ubiquitous BBC Micro which monitors the traffic and performance of the PADs around UWIST and provides a warning when problems occur. It also allows us to measure the extent to which the network is being utilised, and to pinpoint possible trouble spots.

1.8 The future

In the next 5–10 years we envisage a gradual return to manufacturer provided communications software, as ISO standards for File and Job transfer emerge. The part that UWIST has played in the UK in developing communications software has however been useful, both to the academic community, where the VAX is a very popular machine, and to ourselves, because a major proportion of the funding for the UWIST networks has come from sales of our software worldwide.

CHAPTER 2

The use of JANET for the Transfer of Medical Images and Other Files Over a Wide Area Network

R E Bentley, S Webb, A Davies, J Sutcliffe* and P Wild†
*Physics Department, Institute of Cancer Research, *Medical Physics Department, University of Leeds and †MRC Mineral Metabolism Unit, University of Leeds*

2.1 Introduction

It has been said that the 1960s were the decade of mainframes, the 1970s were the decade of minis and micros and the 1980s are the decade of networks. The interconnection of computers into networks is now very common and a large amount of work is being carried out in many centres to provide standardised, efficient, error free procedures both for local area networks (generally within single sites up to about 2.5 km in extent) and wide area networks which may be of any size and operate over circuits provided by Post and Telephone authorities.

There are many reasons for providing links from one computer to another, such as:

1. Local computer is too slow
2. Local computer has insufficient disk space
3. Local computer does not have the required software
4. Local computer does not have the required data
5. Local computer does not have the required peripherals e.g. printers and plotters.

Remote operation may also provide a more convenient way of running bench marks, of comparing the accuracy of different machines, and of sorting out bugs by comparing two supposedly similar computers. Also, the usefulness of electronic mail is much enhanced when computers are connected together.

Four modes of use can be identified:

1. Remote login
2. File transfer
3. Electronic mail, which might be regarded as a special case of file transfer
4. Remote job submission.

2.2 The Joint Academic Network

Examples of practical use of the first three of these modes will be given using JANET (Joint Academic Network), a wide area network administered by the universities and the Science and Engineering Research Council (SERC). JANET uses X25 packet switching protocols over private circuits leased from British Telecom (BT). The method of working is similar to the Packet Switching Service (PSS) of BT and gateways between JANET and PSS have been installed. Most university computer centres, many departmental computers (VAX's and equivalent), and many SERC sites (especially the Rutherford-Appleton Laboratory) are connected to it. In addition, there is a direct link to CERN and

7

there are gateways, provided at present by courtesy of IBM (UK) Ltd., to EARN (European Academic Research Network), BITNET (Because It's There NETwork) in the United States and NETNORTH in Canada. Connection is in progress or being negotiated with polytechnics and Medical Research Council sites.

The VAX 11/750 installed in the section of Physics at the Institute of Cancer Research, for research into image processing and display has been connected to JANET since December 1985. The interface with the X25 protocols is by a software package known as Packetnet System Interface (PSI), supplied by the Digital Equipment Company (DEC), which runs under the VAX operating system VMS. Use of the network is managed by software which runs over PSI, the so-called 'Coloured Books Software' written for the Joint Network Team (JNT) by a group at UWIST and now distributed by DEC. The naming of this software arises from the original JNT specifications: Terminal Protocols in 'The Green Book', Transport Service in 'The Yellow Book', File Transfer in 'The Blue Book', Electronic Mail in 'The Grey Book' and Job Manipulation and Transfer in 'The Red Book'.

2.3   Examples

2.3.1   Transfer of medical images

Experimental data were obtained from a series of 2-dimensional (2D) projections using a cone-beam CT scanner at Leeds. Analysis programs and a display system (Sigmex Args 7000 series) were available on the VAX at Sutton[1]. The raw data were transmitted to the VAX from a PRIME computer at Leeds, also connected to JANET and running the Prime version of the Coloured Books software. This was done by typing the appropriate commands at Sutton to 'fetch' the files from Leeds. Each 2D projection contained 128 x 128 pixels of 4 bytes; 120 projections were transferred, making a total of 7.9 Mbytes of image data. File transmission ended within four hours of requesting that the data file be sent. After allowing for software overheads and the possibility of congestion in the network, this is consistent with the speed of our 7200 bit s^{-1} synchronous link to JANET.

This procedure has the advantage not only of avoiding the delays in packing and posting magnetic media, but also avoids the problem of converting the file format from one machine to another. This is done as a matter of course by the 'Coloured Book' software.

2.3.2   Transatlantic Mail

Co-authorship of scientific papers and other documents is simplified by sending drafts as text files by electronic mail. Whilst Telex and other public electronic mail services may be as fast, use of JANET by persons who have terminals on which they log in regularly provides a service which is easy and convenient to use and gives on-line notification of the receipt of incoming messages. The link through EARN and NETNORTH has been successfully used in communication with Carleton University and the National Research Council, both in Ottawa. A major advantage compared with Telex is that received mail is in a form that may be edited by the recipient and returned to the sender or forwarded elsewhere, locally or within JANET.

2.3.3   Software updates

This is a particularly valuable application which can save much time. We make considerable use of the Starlink image processing package developed by a consortium of astronomy departments and maintained by the Rutherford-Appleton Laboratory. This is a huge package extending in all to some 50 Mbytes, and sub-divided into a very large number of separate VAX files. Updates are made on an individual file basis with some files being modified about once a fortnight. Despatch of magnetic media to all participating sites would be a considerable administrative task. The procedure, therefore, consists of a mail message broadcast to all interested sites and the onus is then on the receiving site to 'fetch' the required files from the maintaining site. Suppliers of commercial software for medical physics requirements, such as systems for radiotherapy planning, nuclear medicine, CT etc. have a similar logistical problem and have as a result sometimes been slow in updating software. These problems could be solved using a network of this kind, though JANET itself may only be used for non-commercial purposes.

2.3.4 Remote login to test array processors

We are currently evaluating different array processors as a means of speeding up various image processing calculations as this is much easier when such a device can be accessed directly. A Floating Point System FPS 5205 is attached to a VAX 11/780 at Kings College, University of London and this machine is also on JANET. We have been able to transfer Fortran files, then login to the 11/780 remotely and use the cross compiler to produce code which is then run on the array processor. Results can be transferred back to our own VAX, and displayed on the Sigmex display system.

2.4 Quality of service

From the users' point of view, an acceptable network should have a number of attributes which include the following:

1. conversion of file format between computers of different type
2. automatic routing, so that the user does not have to be concerned with the actual path of his or her connection, as in a telephone call
3. automatic reconnection, if necessary by an alternative route, in the event of a break in the circuit
4. periodic re-tries at predetermined intervals, when connection fails for any reason
5. notification of completed file transfer and of arrival of new mail
6. notification of failed mail and file transfer
7. very low error rate (of the order of 1 byte in 10^8 to 10^9)
8. should be minimal overhead on the host computer, i.e. should use as little CPU time as possible.

We feel that all of these requirements, except the last one, have been satisfactorily met. Unfortunately the Coloured Books software does place a significant load on a VAX 11/750 and, if used a lot, a significant amount of CPU time would be consumed.

The present system with a maximum transfer rate of 9600 bit s^{-1} is not intended as a routine tool for the analysis of remotely generated images, as it is clearly too slow. We have however, illustrated the value of JANET as a means of carrying out a 'one off' collaborative project between two specific sites and the same should be true of any other pair of randomly selected JANET sites.

9

2.5 The future

Developments in JANET will allow operation over British Telecom Kilostream links up to 64 kbit s^{-1}. This will be a significant improvement for the transfer of image data.

It is to be hoped that more departments of medical physics, especially those affiliated to universities, will be able to link up to JANET. When a significant number of connections have been made, a valuable facility for the transfer of programs, data files and documents will be available to the medical physics community.

Acknowledgements

We wish to thank Ms Sharon Richardson of Carleton University, Ottawa for help in using the link with NETNORTH, Mike Lawdon of the Rutherford-Appleton Laboratory for help in the updating of Starlink files and Nigel Arnot of Kings College, London for permission to use the VAX 11/780 and array processor.

Reference

1   Webb S, Sutcliffe J, Burkinshaw L and Horsman A 1987 Tomographic reconstruction from experimentally-obtained cone-beam projections. *IEEE Trans Med Imaging* **MI6** 67–73

CHAPTER 3

A Computer Network Using the Cambridge Ring and Other Hardware

D L Plummer
Department of Medical Physics and Bioengineering, University College Hospital, London

3.1 Background

The department of medical physics at University College Hopsital (UCH) and University College London (UCL) has several mini-computers and personal computers (PCs) under its control. These range from processors dedicated to particular tasks to general purpose systems providing word processing, data processing etc. It was recognised some years ago that use of PCs, at that time mostly BBC micros, was increasing and that there was a demand for simple data transfer between these machines and other facilities. Also the difficulties of transferring data between larger systems with different operating software created a demand for a local network of some type.

A large proportion of the minicomputer systems involved were DEC PDP11 machines and, had this been exclusively the case, DECNET would have been a strong contender. The need to connect PCs and non-DEC equipment, however, led us to seek an alternative, more open-ended, solution. At that time the present range of low cost character-orientated networks was not available and Ethernet, though clearly an established hardware standard, was both expensive and lacking in software standardisation. Within the British academic community the Cambridge Ring had gained a significant popularity, and several campus networks had been installed. The principal manufacturers of Cambridge Ring hardware were not at that time marketing any software but, with several university systems in operation, the availability of appropriate software was not expected to be a problem.

3.2 The Cambridge Ring

The Cambridge Ring[1,2] is a local area network based on a 10 Mbit s^{-1} dataway connecting up to 254 access nodes in a closed ring. The physical medium for the ring is a single cable of two twisted pairs carrying composite clock and data signals and also power for the ring repeaters, one of which is associated with each node. The design is such that no power is required from the nodes in order to maintain ring integrity. A constant number of fixed-size data packets circulate continuously round the ring, each packet being marked either full or empty. When one node wishes to transmit data to another, it waits for an empty packet, inserts the data and destination address and allows the packet to continue round the ring. Each node examines the destination address of every packet passing and empties those addressed to it. A special node on the ring, the monitor, empties packets that make a complete circuit without being received. The ring packet size is 40 bits, of which 16 are data and 24 are address, error check and flag information. The effective hardware data rate is thus 4 Mbit s^{-1}.

11

Messages are transmitted between nodes in variable length bursts of ring packets known as basic blocks. Nodes have the capacity to select a single packet source and thus, having received the first packet of a block, a node can lock onto its source for the remainder. The basic block structure includes a header pattern, address information and a 16 bit cyclic redundancy check (CRC), in addition to the data. The consecutive ring packets of a block are required to arrive within a short time interval of one another so that blocks truncated by errors can be readily detected. The probability of a ring data error is low, thus it is acceptable to rely on a passive rather than active error correction scheme. Truncated blocks and those with bad CRC are ignored and a timeout mechanism is used in the higher level protocols to request re-transmission of unreceived blocks.

3.3 Software implementation

Although several Cambridge Ring protocol implementations were in existence at the time, none of these seemed to meet our requirements for a system which could readily be transported onto a variety of hosts or, indeed, which existed in a packaged and documented form. It was thus reluctantly decided to exacerbate this situation by developing our own implementation using derivations of the published Cambridge protocols. The initial aim was to connect two PDP11s, one running RT11 and another RSX. The first of these was essentially a dedicated communications node for Remote Job Entry access to central University of London computing facilities, and the second a PDP11/34 general purpose system used for data preparation. The need to produce software that would run on a small machine in parallel with the existing, quite large, communications program was a severe constraint. However it eventually proved possible to write a single program in C that could be compiled conditionally for the environments of RSX, RT11 and UNIX, and that could meet the space requirements[3].

Whilst the cost of connecting a system to the ring (about £1000) is a small fraction of the cost of a minicomputer, the connection of PCs is proportionately much more expensive and, in many cases, the interface hardware is not available. For this reason we included a 16 channel serial line multiplexer as one node in the network so that almost any machine could be connected via RS232. The multiplexer, which contains a 64K Z80 CPU, functions as a switch at the basic block level and routes incoming blocks to either a serial line or a ring node according to the address contained within the block. The software to control this function is loaded into the multiplexer from any other node via the ring when the system is started up.

A file transfer utility was developed in BASIC for use on PCs and proved to be reasonably transportable, requiring only the addition of serial port drivers for each particular machine. Using interrupt driven receivers with pre-allocated buffers, no hardware flow control is required and three wire connection at 9600 baud is possible. As parameters such as timeout intervals and block sizes are negotiated between communicating nodes at the time connection is established, systems with widely different capabilities can use a common hardware link efficiently.

3.4 Network evolution

Figure 3.1 shows the present configuration of the network. It will be seen that only two systems plus the multiplexer are directly connected to the ring and that many transactions can be conducted without ring access. This reflects the independence of the higher level protocols from the underlying link hardware. With this type of

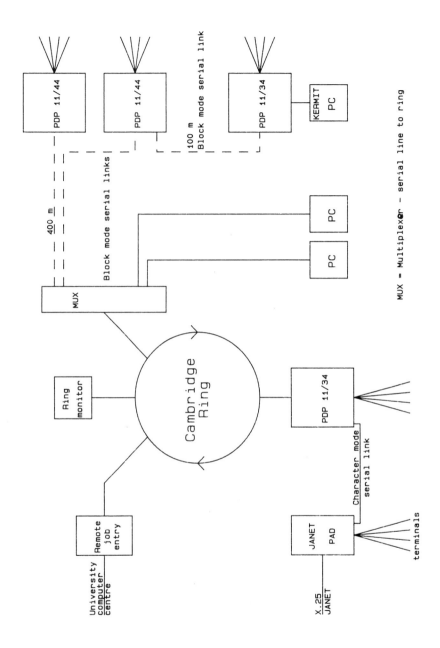

Figure 3.1 Configuration of UCH/UCL network showing the combination of Cambridge Ring and serial links. All internal links carry the same protocol, except for the character bridge to the PAD. Use of the serial multiplexer (MUX) reduces connection costs.

13

configuration, high and low data rate links can be mixed freely in order to achieve a satisfactory compromise of cost and speed.

The serial 9600 baud links from the multiplexer to the machines at the remote sites were added as a temporary measure until it became practical to lay ring cable over the 400 m route. In many cases these transfers are of files for submission to remote batch queues and short delays are acceptable. In fact running at 9600 baud these links have proved sufficiently fast for most purposes and there has been little demand for enhancement. The network processors in the minicomputers are all capable of carrying out multiple transactions and hence a long transfer to a slow PC will not unduly delay another transfer.

At first it was intended to provide only file transfer facilities over the network. This was implemented successfully and found to provide a reliable service. The possibility of providing network terminal access was considered but was initially expected to be too slow over the 9600 baud serial links for which it would be most useful. After running the file transfer service for some time it was decided to attempt an experimental terminal service and this was implemented with some slight extensions to the protocols to provide a full duplex connection. The results were most rewarding as, even multiplexed on a 9600 baud serial line with other communications, a useful connection could be maintained.

At the time the network was first commissioned it was difficult to predict usage patterns. The initial implementation was mainly experimental and facilities were offered to users on an 'as found' basis. In a matter of months users had found numerous reasons for transferring files between systems: remote job submission, working on the least busy machine, distribution of updates to system and application software, independence of system down time etc. At present the network carries approximately 100 transactions (a total of 1 Mbyte) per week.

The terminal service was initially envisaged as a means of accessing local systems for which no directly connected terminal was available. However the presence of a JANET (Joint Academic NETwork—see 2.2) PAD (Packet Assembler Disassembler) adjacent to one node made open-systems connection possible and it was found to be practical to call over the ring network to the PAD and out onto JANET. Such connections suffer from the limitations of a simple character bridge between the ring network and the X25 PAD. Connection attributes can only be set by dialogue directly with the PAD and cannot be forced by the overall call. File transfer can only be achieved by character copy facilities built into the ring software and no standard network File Transfer Protocol is available. For these reasons the network remains rather limited for open-systems access.

3.5 Performance

3.5.1 Performance monitoring

To facilitate performance monitoring, the software in the multi-user nodes was written so as to accumulate statistics on the size and duration of transfers, and also to record the nature of any errors. This permits both a detailed analysis of the performance of the various connections and enables the possibility of detecting some hardware problems in their early stages.

3.5.2 Data transfer rates

The majority of data transferred between our systems consists of small files and, even on the relatively slow 9600 baud lines, the transfer rates are sufficient.

Typical data rates over these links are 250 byte s^{-1}. As a major part of the transfer time is the overhead in executing the protocol in the end nodes of the connection, actual data rates fall far short of the physical link capability. The mean data rate on a direct ring connection is 375 byte s^{-1} compared with a link capability of 500 000 byte s^{-1}. One factor affecting the transmission rate is the basic block size; the upper limit on this is determined by the availability of buffer space in the nodes and the need to keep the probability of an error within a block low. A second factor, and probably the most important one, is the limited CPU time generally available in a multi-user system. Execution speed of the protocol is severely limited, and to approach full utilisation of the ring band width it is necessary to execute the protocol in a dedicated front end processor.

There are noticeable limitations for terminal connections on slow lines, particularly when using programs such as editors which require single character interaction. For those applications that require only line by line interaction the network delays are usually swamped by the remote system response time.

3.5.3 Error rates

Error rates on both the ring and the serial lines have been found to be higher than expected. On a pure ring connection the rate is approximately 18 in 10^6. On the serial lines it can be as high as 160 in 10^6 but a significant proportion of these errors may be due to character loss on input to heavily loaded RSX systems. These rates do not present any problems to the user as the error detection system is highly effective and the probability of an undetected error is negligible. In use the system may occasionally fail to transfer a file if the destination system is very heavily loaded, but the user is guaranteed that if the data arrives at all it is correct. The overall transfer failure rate is under five per cent.

3.5.4 File formats

One aim of the system was to provide a convenient means of transferring files between different system types. To accommodate the various record formats existing on the systems it was decided to adopt a standard format for transfer on the network and to convert to and from this locally. We chose the C/UNIX convention of using the linefeed character as a record separator. This precludes the transmission of binary files and some documents with special printer formatting. An alternative mode was thus implemented in which a pure binary image of the file could be sent together with a small quantity of system dependent attribute information. This enables object files to be transmitted between like systems, and also allows word processor output to be sent to a central machine for printing.

3.5.5 Large data sets

The present system makes no attempt to compress data for transmission. The architecture is essentially context independent and to incorporate a useful compression scheme would require a significant amount of prior knowledge of the data. We have investigated various compression techniques for images and this is discussed elsewhere[4]. If required, compression can be applied prior to transmission as part of a system command macro.

3.5.6 Security

No discussion of networking should avoid this issue which, in medical applications, is of particular concern. Networking presents two main threats to data security. Firstly, if systems are accessible from remote terminals, the physical access controls which provide the principal element of security are removed. Secondly, as data may be transferred over cables in public or readily accessible positions, there is always the possibility of illicit tapping into the system. Unwanted access from remote terminals can be limited by using appropriately secure software and ensuring that IDs and passwords are kept confidential. The present network validates the user identification before giving access to a remote file. Physical interception within the network hardware is much less probable but can only be protected against by encrypting data. We have not felt it necessary to adopt this tactic yet as at present our transfer of sensitive data is limited. In the future, however, we may need to introduce encryption as part of the network system.

3.6   Future developments

Our experiences with the Cambridge Ring have taught us a great deal about the usage of a local area network in our environment. Through implementing a system and tailoring it to our specific needs we have identified those factors on which we depend most, and have been in a position to monitor use and performance better than would have been possible with a commercial package. We recognise that the development of communications software is time consuming and thus expensive and that network software and hardware are now becoming available to meet most requirements. We are now looking to the future and the possibility of installing an 'off the shelf' supported system. The experience with the ring has enabled us to develop a realistic specification for this next generation of network hardware and software.

Primarily our requirement is for a simple, and not neccessarily very fast, file transfer between systems. The advent of KERMIT has reduced the problems in transfer between PCs and it is now common practice to KERMIT files onto a local processor and then dispatch them elsewhere with the Ring network. This has greatly reduced our need to connect PCs to the general network although for some applications this remains useful. Larger workstation type systems fall into this class.

As network transfers on the minicomputer systems are initiated by system commands, they can also be performed from within programs. This has been found useful for sending output to a local printer when physically connected to a remote system. A simple electronic mail system was also developed using this capability. Whilst this ability to initiate and wait for network file transfers is useful, we have found no demand for true network file access. The tendency has been toward PCs with substantial local storage rather than dependence on a central file server. In the future, the advent of diskless workstations and the need for multi-user access to the file base may create a requirement for this function.

Although there is direct terminal access to at least two systems in our main work areas, the terminal connection facility of the network is useful both for access to our own systems and to external services. Though limited in its scope and inefficient in implementation, the possibility of making terminal calls has proved most valuable. Distributed terminal access is thus a requirement. It can be achieved either, as in our system, by software within the nodes or by using terminal multiplexers connected directly to the network.

We are currently reviewing our requirements with a view to substantially increasing both our processing power and our communication capabilities. Though we have made a significant investment in Cambridge Ring hardware and software, this has been amply repaid in the form of our understanding of the potential for use of a local network. We will now be looking at commercial configurations, probably based on Ethernet, to provide a comparable configuration in a fully supported form. By installing an X25 gateway on one system we will be able to improve our access to remote systems over JANET and hence provide better facilities for collaboration with other departments and centres.

There will certainly be features in this new system which exceed those limited requirements specified above, and it is probable that we will learn to exploit their full potential in time. Having evaluated our requirements within an inherently flexible system, it should be possible to select a new system that will provide a useful service immediately.

References

1   Wilkes M V and Wheeler D J 1979 The Cambridge Digital Communication Ring *Proc. US National Bureau of Standards Symposium on Local Area Networks* (Boston MA)
2   Wheeler D J and Hopper A 1979 Maintenance of Ring Communications Systems *IEEE Trans. on Communications* **COM-27** 760
3   Plummer D L and Chandarana R H 1983 *UCL Clinical Sciences Communication Software* UCL Medical Physics internal report.
4   Todd-Pokropek A, Chan C and Appledorn R 1986 Image data compression techniques applicable to image networks, in *Information Processing in Medical Imaging* (ed S L Bacharach) (Martinus Nijhoff, Dordrecht, Netherlands)

CHAPTER 4

Data Compression Techniques for the Transmission of Images

A Todd-Pokropek
Department of Medical Physics, University College London

4.1 Introduction

Digitally acquired images are being used more often in medical diagnosis. There is an associated need to transmit them over image networks, both high speed networks as might be present within a hospital complex, and slower networks linking hospital to hospital, or general practice group to hospital. At present, all images obtained in CT, MRI, DSA, and most images in nuclear medicine and ultrasound exist in digital form. Much of conventional radiology, when appropriate captors have been developed, will also have the capability of being performed digitally, albeit using rather large matrix sizes. The availability of images in digital form lend themselves to the use of image processing for enhancement, and digital long term storage, and should make retrieval more reliable.

But for such a system to be (financially) viable, it is necessary that access to such digital images, and the means to manipulate them, be widely available. An image network (with appropriate image workstations) must be created. However, a major limitation in most current PACS (Picture Archiving and Communication System) networks is that they tend to be limited to a small geographical area, and work at very high data rates. For example the ACR/NEMA interface specifications[1] suggest data rates of ~ 80 Mbits s^{-1}. Such rates cannot be maintained over long distances, and therefore cannot be used for a wide area network. The efficient use of low speed links to a wide area network implies the use of data compression, although data compression may also be useful for archiving. For example, if a raw image was ~ 0.5 Mbytes in size, then the time to transmit this typical image would be ~ 200 s, at a data transmission rate of 19.2 kbaud. A highly desirable data compression ratio would be to reduce this time by a factor of 100, corresponding to ~ 0.1–0.2 bits/pixel in the compressed image.

Descriptions of some particular systems are given in references 2–4 and many other general references may be found in reference 5. Such studies indicate that a data compression ratio of about 10 (to achieve ~ 1 bit/pixel) can be achieved to make suitable use of data communication channels, but that considerable processing power may be required at both transmitting and receiving station. An excellent general review of data compression is given by Jain[6], and in the chapter on data compression in Rosenfeld and Kak[7]. Both papers contain many further references to the data compression literature. A more recent review is that of Kunt et al[8].

4.2 Entropy — a lower limit

Consider the transmission of a series of symbols over some (noisy) line in order to transmit information about the *source* to the *receiver*. Information theory suggests that, for continuous additive functions (which are linear and homogeneous) a

18

suitable measure of the information $I(a_j)$ that has been gained when a symbol has been received is

$$I(a_j) = -\log(\mathbf{P}[a_j]) \qquad (1)$$

where $\mathbf{P}[a_j]$ is the probability of occurrence of a symbol a_j within an alphabet $\{\mathbf{a}\}$ (and a natural logarithm is usually employed to give information in units called 'nats'). Its expected value is called the entropy H such that

$$H = -\sum_j \mathbf{P}[a_j] \log(\mathbf{P}[a_j]) \qquad (2)$$

where the summation is over all possible symbols a_j.

Thus B_{max}, the *maximum* number of bits needed to be transmitted for an image (excluding identification information etc) is the number of pixels, for example N × N, assuming the image is square, multiplied by the number of bits/pixel N_{max}. For example, in a conventional CT image this is 512 × 512 × 16 bits, i.e. 0.5 Mbytes or 4 Mbits.

One value for the *lower* limit is defined by the entropy[6,7]. Let $\mathbf{P}[i]$ be the probability that a given pixel takes the value i; then zero order entropy H_0 is defined as

$$H_0 = -\sum_i \mathbf{P}[i] \log_2(\mathbf{P}[i]) \qquad (3)$$

where effectively the alphabet $\{\mathbf{a}\}$ has been restricted to integers between 0 and N_{max}, and following the convention in computing, a base 2 logarithm has been substituted to give the result for H_0 in bits. A typical value reported for a CT image is about 6 bits/pixel[6]. A data compression technique which achieves the limit suggested by zero order entropy could compress such a conventional CT image from 4 Mbits to about 1.5 Mbits, that is, achieve a compression of just over a factor of 2. Huffman coding can come very close to achieving such compression[6].

Let N_{pix} be the average number of bits required after compression of an image containing N × N pixels. Compression ratios are often defined in terms of the ratio of B_{max} to N × N × N_{pix}. However, for the rest of this paper, the efficiency of data compression techniques will be considered only in terms of the average number of bits per pixel after compression (N_{pix}). The use of 'compression ratios' can sometimes be rather misleading since they depend on B_{max}, which can artificially be increased. For Gaussian distributed data (here the pixel values), it may be shown that entropy is, to a good approximation, independent of N_{max} (the maximum number of bits/pixel), although very dependent on the variance. Entropy is only small when the variance is very small. This provides support for expressing compression in terms of bits/pixel (N_{pix}) rather than as a compression ratio.

Shannon's noiseless coding theorem states that it is possible to code without distortion a source (of many pixels) of entropy H using H + ϵ data bits[6,7], where ϵ is a constant arbitrarily close to zero. Under certain constraints, zero order entropy would appear to be the absolute lower limit for compression. Firstly, the image data is assumed to be formed from independent Gaussian variables, and therefore completely decorrelated. Secondly, it is assumed that the compression needs to be completely reversible, that is, the original image can *identically* be reconstructed after expansion of the compressed image. However, firstly, most medical images have very considerable correlation between pixel values. Secondly, if the compressed image after expansion cannot be *distinguished* from the original image, although not strictly identical, such a compression method would normally be considered acceptable. Both these facts lead to the exploitation of data compression methods which can give a value of bits per pixel very much less than that suggested from zero order entropy. Whether such data compression methods will be considered acceptable by clinicians is a separate issue.

First order entropy H_1 is given by

$$H_1 = \sum_{i_1} \sum_{i_2} \mathbf{P}[i_1 \mid i_2] \log_2 \mathbf{P}[i_1 \mid i_2] \tag{4}$$

where $\mathbf{P}[i_1 \mid i_2]$ is the conditional probabability of state i_1 given state i_2, and higher order entropies are H_n defined correspondingly using n states. Typical values quoted for H_1 and H_2 are 4 and 2 bits respectively for CT data. This gives some indication of the potential for compression by exploiting the correlation between pixels.

A basic tool of data compression techniques is to eliminate the co-variance between pixels, and to transmit only the independent component, which is essentially the random variations between the expected image and the observed image. As might be expected, in medical images, such random variations are mostly (but not entirely) noise. Thus if noise may be suppressed (which is therefore non-reversible), very efficient data compression can be achieved.

Finally, from a theoretical point of view, the rate distortion function[9] R gives a fairly complete description of any communication channel. R is the minimum value of mutual information as a function of that threshold of distortion that is defined as acceptable, see for example Kak[7]. It is essentially the minimal channel capacity that must be available in order to ensure that the distortion will never be greater than some limit. Unfortunately, while the rate distortion function provides a good conceptual handling of the limits of data compression, it is almost impossible to compute and therefore remains primarily of theoretical interest.

4.3 Fidelity

If an image is transmitted in a non-reversible manner, for example when images are transmitted over noisy lines and errors occur, some measure of how far away the transmitted image is from the original is required. No distance measure currently used appears to be completely satisfactory for medical images.

Let $x(i,j)$ be a pixel in the original image, and $x'(i,j)$ be a pixel in the image after compression and restoration (which we will call the 'transmitted' image). Most fidelity measures are based on a least squares estimate, for example, of the form for the average mean squared error e^2_{ms} such that

$$e^2_{ms} = \frac{1}{N^2} \sum_i \sum_j E\left\{ (x(i,j) - x'(i,j))^2 \right\} \tag{5}$$

where $\{E\}$ is the expected value, and the image is assumed to be square of side length N. The sample mean square error e'^2_{ms}, which is in fact often used, is exactly the same as for e^2_{ms}, but using the observed squared difference rather than its expectation.

Related to these two error estimates are definitions of signal to noise ratios (SNRs) which may be expressed either in dBs or as pure ratios. For example peak-to-peak SNR may be expressed as

$$SNR = 10\log_{10}\left[\frac{(MAX\text{-}MIN)^2}{e^2_{ms}} \right] dB \tag{6}$$

where MAX-MIN is the peak to peak difference in the original image. A commonly used form for MAX-MIN is just the total range of values in the image, e.g. the largest possible integer. A better estimate of signal might be considered to be the variance σ^2_x from which an alternative definition of SNR can be defined as

$$\text{SNR}' = 10\log_{10}\left(\frac{\sigma^2_x}{e^2_{ms}}\right) \text{dB} \qquad (7)$$

All these least square error based estimates have the usual problem of being sensitive to gross changes in the image and insensitive to local changes.

Some attempts have been made to use measures based on some visual perception criterion. For example Mannos and Sakirson[10] have proposed a weighted mean square contrast error as follows. Let f( ) be some non-linear function. Let $c(i,j)$ be an estimate of contrast change at the point i,j such that

$$c(i,j) = f(\ x(i,j) - x'(i,j)\ ) \qquad (8)$$
$$\text{and } C(u,v) = F\{c(i,j)\}$$

where $F\{\ \}$ is the 2-D Fourier transform, and let e^2_c be the mean squared error in contrast defined as

$$e^2_c = \int \int |\ C(u,v)\ H(u,v)\ |^2 \ du\ dv \qquad (9)$$

where $H(u,v)$ is the chosen weighting function. It is interesting to note that Mannos and Sakirson suggest using

$$f(u) = u^{1/3}$$

but if H is assumed to be circularly symmetric then

$$H(u,v) = H(w)$$

and a specific model is

$$H(w) = A\ (a + (w/w_0)^\alpha)\ \exp(-(\ (w/w_0)^\beta) \qquad (10)$$

with appropriate constants for A, a, α, β and w_0 where w is radial distance. This is a separable exponential model, and is often assumed in various data compression models and also when performing Wiener type filtering operations.

Another measure often used is based on the χ^2 distance, where the least squares difference is normalized with respect to the variance, with a general form of the type

$$\chi^2 = \sum_i \sum_j \left[\frac{|\ (x(i,j) - x'(i,j)\ |^2}{\sigma^2}\right] \qquad (11)$$

where σ is defined in an appropriate (local or global manner) with respect to the original image. The variance (expected at a point) is sometimes included within the summation.

In summary, it is clear that, as compression increases, so fidelity is likely to become worse, in exactly the same manner as expected for the rate distortion function. No single fidelity measure has been found to be ideal. A few more empirical methods are helpful, or even essential. It is useful to display the difference image, i.e. $d(i,j) = x(i,j) - x'(i,j)$ as a function of compression. It is also helpful to use ROC methods comparing data before and after compression to check whether any (significant) loss of information has occurred, or if any difference in interpretation of the image would result.

4.4 The KL transform

In the discrete case the Karhunen-Loeve (KL) transform is defined by the relationship

$$F(u,v) = \sum_m \sum_n f(m,n) \, \Phi^{(u,v)*}(m,n) \tag{12}$$

and its inverse by

$$f(m,n) = \sum_u \sum_v F(u,v) \, \Phi^{(u,v)}(m,n) \tag{13}$$

where $f(m,n)$ is the original image, $F(u,v)$ is the transformed image, where the basis functions $\Phi^{(u,v)}$ are a set of orthonormal matrices or eigenmatrices, of which $\Phi^{(u,v)}(p,q)$ is the (p,q)th element. These eigenmatrices are given from the solution of

$$\sum_p \sum_q R(m,n,p,q) \, \Phi^{(u,v)}(p,q) = \Gamma_{uv} \, \Phi^{(u,v)}(m,n) \tag{14}$$

where R is the autocorrelation function

$$R(m,n,p,q) = E\left\{ f(m,n) \, f^*(p,q) \right\} \tag{15}$$

$$\Gamma_{uv} = E\left\{ |F(u,v)|^2 \right\} \tag{16}$$

and $E\{\ \}$ indicates the expected value. In this case it may be shown that

$$E\left\{ F(u,v) \, F^*(u',v') \right\} = 0 \quad \text{for } u \neq u' \; v \neq v' \tag{17}$$

since $E\{F(u,v)\}=0$ provided that $E\{f(m,n)\}=0$, i.e. that the original images had a mean value of zero. This is the desired result, in that the correlations of the transformed image are expected to be zero.

In this sense, the Karhunen-Loeve (KL) transform is therefore optimal in generating uncorrelated values from an image with correlated pixels. Thus the KL transform can be used to generate the set of values $F(m,n)$ with minimum entropy, which is, in this sense, optimal for data compression. However, the use of the KL transform itself is image dependent. Strictly, it must be recomputed for every image, and is therefore computationally not very convenient, requiring N^4 operations for N^2 coefficients. It is desirable to look for alternatives or approximations. One approximation has been employed to generate a so-called Fast KL transform, which is based on an image model of the form given by equation (10). The derivation of a fast KL transform is well described by Kak[7].

4.5 Other transforms

Another suitable approximation which is much easier to implement than the KL transform, is the use of the discrete cosine transform (DCT), defined as

$$F(u,v) = \frac{4\,c(u,v)}{N^2} \sum_n \sum_m f(m,n) \cos(\,(2m+1)\,\pi u \,/\, 2N) \cos(\,(2n+1)\,\pi v \,/\, 2N) \tag{18}$$

where $c(u,v) = 0.5$ for $u=v=0$ and 1 elsewhere. It may be demonstrated that, for a small matrix size of 16×16, the basis functions of the DCT transform are very close to those of the KL transform[11], where, as before, the autocorrelation matrix is assumed to be separable and to obey an exponential model as in equation (10).

The advantage of using the DCT over the KL transform is primarily that of computational efficiency. The DCT can also be implemented using a conventional FFT with appropriate weights, and in addition there is a fast form of the transform available[11]. When the image is decomposed into blocks of size n × n (see below) the DCT also has a symmetry property over 2n which tends to reduce the so called blocking artefact (where the edges between blocks may be visible in the image after compression). Most data compression methods reported in the applied literature have used the DCT compression.

Another transform which may be used is the S transform[12,13], closely related to the Hadamard transform. Although this transform does not in fact compress the total amount of data, it may be employed to transmit firstly a low resolution copy of the original image, followed by the transmission of additional data to restore the image (at leisure) to its full resolution. This is of considerable value in terms of improving the apparent response time of image transmission, and thereby improving its efficiency.

4.6 Discretization, encoding and blocking

Having performed some transformation, one is left with a series of real (essentially continuous) values which are inappropriate for transmission. These values must be turned into symbols, that is, located with respect to a set of discrete intervals, a process known as 'discretization'. The simplest form of such an operation is to convert the real numbers into integers. However, the range of values found after use of the transform have typically very different (dynamic) ranges. The fundamental is usually very large, but higher order coefficients fall off very rapidly. The choice of an appropriate encoding scheme can achieve significant gains in compression for given noise properties.

Normally, it is found very inefficient to manipulate the whole image (which might be of size 1k × 1k) in a single operation, and the image is usually treated as a series of blocks of size n × n, for example 16 × 16. Non square blocks may also be employed. However, it is important that after transmission the edges between blocks should not generate (blocking) artefacts; and that the selection of values be chosen to given good decorrelation after the transform[14].

Optimal codes may be selected by studying the performance of the transform for many samples of image data. Essentially Huang and Schultheiss[15] have performed a constrained minimization and obtained the result that

$$b(u,v) = b_{aver} - 0.5 \log_2(\sigma^2(u,v)) - \frac{1}{2n^2} \sum_u \sum_v \log_2(\sigma^2(u,v)) \tag{19}$$

where $\sigma^2(u,v)$ is the expected variance at the position, u,v in the n × n transform, $b(u,v)$ is the number of bits used to encode the data at that position, and b_{aver} is the desired average number of bits/pixel.

An alternative method of transmitting part of the data, after transformation, at full precision (using all the bits), while eliminating other terms in certain blocks dependent on the 'information' present in each block, has been described by Elnahas et al[16] who claim improvements of 17dB in signal to noise ratio over other conventional methods.

4.7 Run-length and predictive coding

Run length coding (RLC) is often suggested as a suitable data compression technique. In essence, when a pixel value is found to be repeated, RLC consists of recording the value of the pixel and the number of times that it occurs, rather than storing the complete sequence. Thus edges of images when uniformly zero may be largely eliminated, that is, replaced by a zero value and a count. Many improvements can be made. for example by using variable length bit codes to store changes rather than absolute values etc. Unfortunately, the run lengths observed in medical images tend to be very short, when edges are excluded[17]. Much of this is a result of random fluctuations associated with statistical noise.

Predictive coding is, in a way, a related technique. If one knows the expected form of the image, then one can record only the differences between that image, and the observed image[6,7]. Such differences might be expected to be very uncorrelated, and thus very efficient data compression could be achieved. Simple techniques can and have been employed, for example, by predicting the value of the jth pixel horizontally in an image in terms of some linear combination of the previous j-1. . . .j-i pixels. In this case, only the difference between the predicted value and the observed value is recorded, and compression results because of the decrease in the number of bits required to store such a difference, with respect to that of the original pixel value.

Let $f'(m,n)$ be the predicted value, using some rule, at the point m,n and $f(m,n)$ be the actual value. The error $e(m,n)$ is given by

$$e(m,n) = f(m,n) - f'(m,n) \qquad (20)$$

and is the value that needs to be transmitted. For a random field $E\left\{e(m,n)\right\} = 0$. If a similar model for the autocorrelation functions is assumed as in equation(10) then

$$E\left\{e(m,n)e(p,q)\right\} = 0, m \neq p \ n \neq q \qquad (21)$$

and the transmitted values are actually decorrelated as desired. Predictors for $f'(m,n)$ can be horizontal, vertical, linear, non-linear, and include various numbers of terms (previous picture elements), generally called the order of the predictor. Common systems found are first to third order linear horizontal predictors. The simplest form of predictive coding is one using a one step delay, with a one bit quantizer to indicate <greater> or <less> in the comparison between estimation and observation. This form of coding is called delta modulation.

4.8 Pyramid coding

A pyramid may be defined as a set of images G_L where each image is defined by means of some rule, for example summation of adjacent pixels, from the previous image in the pyramid G_{L-1}. The initial image G_0 is the raw data or original image. Burt[18] has described a novel form of data compression using pyramids, and examples are also given in reference 8. A Gaussian pyramid can be constructed in terms of the REDUCE operation, basically a Gaussian blurring, and an EXPAND operation, basically a Gaussian interpolation, both defined more precisely by Burt[18]. Let G_L be one level of such a Gaussian pyramid, after the original image G_0 has been blurred L times. A typical Gaussian blurring function can be generated from a 5×5 smoothing filter with appropriate weights.

A Laplacian pyramid LAP[18] can be created, being a set of images such that the Lth image is given by

$$LAP_L = G_L - EXPAND\ [G_{L+1}] \qquad (22)$$

and

$$G_0 = \sum_L LAP_{L,L} \qquad (23)$$

24

where G_0 is the original image, and the subscript L,L indicates that the Lth image in LAP has been expanded L times. If G_0 is of size $N \times N$ then the entire set of data in LAP may be shown to be $\sim(4/3)N^2$. Thus the operation of creating the Laplacian pyramid will only slightly increase the amount of data (by 1/3).

However, on 'discretization', or encoding, the amount of data can be considerably reduced. The lowest level of the Laplacian pyramid contains mostly noise and can be encoded very coarsely. Higher order pyramids are each reduced in size by a factor of 4 and because of this are therefore less critical. They may then be, and indeed should be, encoded more finely. Burt[18] has suggested using bin sizes of 19,9,5,3 for the four lowest levels of the pyramid for an image with a maximum grey value of 255. Each level of the pyramid corresponds to the equivalent of the result of band pass filtering at progressively lower spatial frequencies. The image can be built up in reverse order, starting with the highest order (smallest) Laplacian pyramid levels, and progressively adding in lower orders containing finer detail. Thus provided the EXPAND operation can be performed rapidly by the display hardware, the image can be recovered in coarse resolution, and resolution progressively improved, while the observer is watching.

Perhaps one of the most attractive features of the pyramid coding method is the similarity between the processing of such multi-resolution image sequences, and one possible mechanism for visual perception. It may be that such a coding scheme is a 'natural' coding scheme in that there is a better mapping between the data structure and the manner in which they are handled by an observer. The pyramid method has some relationship with an old method known as the 'synthetic high' technique, where an image is split into low frequency and high frequency components, the low frequencies encoded very coarsely, the high frequencies being treated essentially as edges[8].

4.9   Directional decomposition

Some other potential methods for improving compression are discussed in reference 8 where the use of a general contour-texture model for coding is recommended as a method for establishing the a-priori model of the image, based on aspects determined from a knowledge of the human visual system.

Let a series of high pass filters $H_i(u,v)$ be defined over some set of angles $\theta(i)$ for some appropriate cut-off frequency. A low frequency image is also generated. Thus after filtering (using an appropriate window function) the set of i directional images are input into a zero crossing detector to find edges (by looking for negative values in the product of adjacent pixels) and their magnitudes. These filtered images may be sampled at coarser intervals, and the positions of edges recorded after Huffman coding[7]. The image is reconstructed by interpolating between edges and adding the low frequency component.

An improvement to the above can be obtained (it is suggested) if pixels are classified into 'contour' pixels, those pixels defining an edge, and 'texture' pixels, those within an edge in some region. This implies, first of all, the use of a preprocessor to remove structure (granularity) within edges, then detecting edges, and then eliminating artefacts. Having segmented the image in that manner, the segments themselves can be encoded, using the raw image, in terms of some texture parameter (such as average run-length). This process can also be performed using a split-merge type of algorithm, or using pyramid type algorithms. Very efficient coding has been claimed[8].

25

4.10　3-D data compression

A dramatic improvement in the data compression efficiency can be achieved when considering not just single images but sets of images either in 3-D, or in time. The compression techniques previously discussed were achieved by predicting structure in 2-D. It appears that elimination of co-variance in the third dimension can, in principle, produce results of up to a factor of ten better, but at the expense of a considerable increase in computational complexity and storage requirements.

One method which has been used is to perform a 3-D DCT block transform over a $16 \times 16 \times 16$ volume, in a manner equivalent to that used for the 2-D 16×16 transform. The major drawback with this method occurs when the number of slices is limited, or resolution is very different along the three spatial axes. One partial solution is to encode data over other volumes, for example $16 \times 16 \times 4$, with some loss of efficiency.

If a 3-D pyramid is constructed, reducing each $2 \times 2 \times 2$ volume to a $1 \times 1 \times 1$ element, the total number of voxels in the entire image is only $\sim(8/7)N^3$ for a 3-D image of side N. Thus there is even less difference in the total number of voxels than for a 2-D pyramid. Laplacian 3-D pyramids can be constructed using an extension of the algorithm given previously, and data compressed correspondingly.

4.11　Some results

Various data compression methods have been tested at University College London, and applied to CT scans of size 256×256, and radioisotope scans of size 64×64. The total number of bits required after compression was noted, and converted to an average value per pixel. The image was then 'decompressed' and compared visually with the original image. A difference image was also generated. Various distance measures where used: an L_2 norm (in fact the RMS error) the X-squared distance, the maximum error, and signal to noise ratio (SNR). The following results were concluded:

1. Reversible noiseless data compression does not seem to be able to achieve useful amounts of data compression. Non-reversible data compression is able to achieve much greater compression without significant (e.g. noticeable) changes in compressed images. The best reversible data compression methods report of the order of 2.5 average bits/pixel.
2. The use of run length coding was not helpful, with the exception of edge stripping, which, on its own, could at almost no cost in computing remove 50% of the data. The best data compression found was similarly about 2.5 average bits/pixel.
3. The DCT transform can give good results, down to $\sim$1.5 bits/pixel, but some blocking artefacts are generated. A full $N \times N$ DCT transform of large matrices may not be computationally convenient.
4. The Laplacian pyramid coding approach is encouraging, can give similar compression as the DCT, and does not generate blocking artefacts. It is rather computer intensive. Using Huffman coding data compression of $\sim$1.0–1.5 average bits/pixel can be achieved.

The compression techniques employed tended to be rather heavy on computation time, for example requiring of the order of several seconds of time ($\sim$30 s for a 256×256 matrix) on a PDP11/44. They can be made more efficient, for example by the use of appropriate hardware such as an array (vector) processor and it is estimated that sub-second compression techniques can be achieved for use with high speed links. Both the DCT and the Laplacian techniques are suitable for handling in this manner. The interest in multi-resolution image processing makes it possible that special hardware for creating and manipulating pyramids may become available.

For low speed bridges, where the computational requirement is less, the use of 80286 or 68020 CPUs should be quite adequate to perform the computation without slowing the link.

4.12 Conclusion

The use of digital information in medical imaging can be exploited to a much greater extent if image data can be widely distributed. This seems to imply the use of low speed bridges for some time into the future, such that compression techniques will be essential for their exploitation. A (near) loss-less coding scheme, or one which only removes noise, even if it achieves a tenfold reduction in the amount of data in images, is only desirable if the computational overheads can be made acceptable. This seems to imply that special purpose hardware must be used.

References

1   ACR/NEMA 1984 Draft report. Digital imaging and communications standard
2   Ackerman L V, Flynn M J, Froelich J W, Zerwelch J P, Lund S R and Block R W 1984 Implementation of a broadband network in a diagnostic radiology department and large hospital. *Radiology* **153(P)** 249
3   DHSS and NWTRHA 1984 *The creation of a film-less radiology department and hospital.* Publication STB/9/84 (DHSS, London)
4   Gitlin J N 1985 Teleradiology, presented at RSNA/AAPM symposium on Electronic Radiology: Image Archival, PACS and Teleradiology. *Radiology* **157(P)** 254
5   Society of Photo-Optical Instrumentation Engineers 1983 *Second International Conference and Workshop on Picture Archiving and Communication Systems (PACS II) for Medical Applications* SPIE Publication **418** (SPIE, Bellingham, Washington, USA)
6   Jain A K 1981 Image data compression: a review. *Proc IEEE* **69** 349–406
7   Rosenfeld A and Kak A C 1982 *Digital Picture Processing* 2nd Edition (Academic Press, New York), Vol 1 Chapter 5.
8   Kunt M, Ikonomopoulos A and Kocker M 1985 Second-generation image coding techniques *Proc IEEE* **73** 549–574
9   Berger T 1971 *Rate distortion theory, a mathematical basis for data compression* (Prentice-hall, Eaglewood Cliffs, New Jersey)
10 Mannos J L and Sakirson D J 1974 The effects of a visual fidelity criterion on the encoding of images *IEEE Trans Inform Theory* **IT-20** 525–536
11 Ahmed N, Natarajan T and Rao K R 1974 Discrete cosine transform *IEEE Trans Comput* **C-25** 90–93
12 Todd-Pokropek A, Chan C and Appledorn A 1986 Image data compression techniques applicable to image networks, in *Information processing in medical imaging* (ed S L Bacharach) pp 522—536 (Martinus Nijhoff, Dordrecht)
13 Lux P 1977 A novel set of closed orthogonal functions for image coding *AEII* **31** 267–274
14 Di Paola R and Todd-Pokropek A E 1981 New developments in techniques for information processing in radionuclide imaging, in *Medical radionuclide imaging* pp 287–312 (IAEA, Vienna)
15 Huang T T Y and Schultheiss P M 1963 Block quantization of correlated Gaussian random variables *IRE Trans Commun. Syst* **CS-11** 289–297
16 Elnahas S E, Tzou K-H, Cox J R, Hill R L and Jost R G 1986 Progressive coding and transmission of digital diagnostic pictures *IEEE Trans. Med. Imaging* **MI-5** 73–83

17   Chan C A 1984 *Data compression of medical images* MSc Dissertation, University College London

18   Burt P J 1984 The pyramid as a structure for efficient computation, in *Multiresolution image processing and analysis* (ed A Rosenfeld) pp 6–37 (Springer-Verlag, Berlin)

CHAPTER 5

Data Collection and Transfer in a District General Hospital Haematology Laboratory

D McG Clarkson and M Gibson*
Departments of Medical Physics and Bioengineering and
*Department of Haematology, Glan Clwyd Hospital, Bodelwyddan, Clwyd

5.1 Introduction

Undoubtedly a major problem in the use of microcomputer systems is that of effective data linkage. Yet whilst total integration using network interconnection[1] may appear the only workable solution, this is not necessarily so in practice. A major reason for this apparent contradiction is the way in which various data collection processes are undertaken. The following example of a haematology laboratory in a 400 bed District General Hospital outlines how working practices can influence the approach to the operation of an information system.

5.2 Why use computers?

The introduction of the first microcomputer into the haematology department in 1980 come with the replacement of an ageing Reporter 7 unit (phase A) by a Cromemco System 3 microcomputer (phase B). This Z-80 based system with twin 1.2 Mbyte eight inch floppy disk drives was interfaced to the BCD output of a Model S Coulter Counter in order to print haematology profiles on sticky labels and display values on a VDU. Although this allowed increased flexibility in the way in which specimens were processed, at this early stage no patient data were stored. It was with the purchase of an additional microcomputer (phase C), a Cromemco System 2 with twin 5¼ inch floppy drives, and the upgrading of the System 3 to incorporate a 5.5 Mbyte Winchester disk, that development of an information system was undertaken. The newly acquired System 2 was in fact relegated to the relatively undemanding task of capturing data from the Coulter counter while the System 3 became the principal data processing unit.

It is perhaps important to outline the main roles for which the system was being developed. The system's prime function was to capture and print the haematology profiles processed by the Coulter counter. This function was undertaken immediately after the process of specimen analysis. The secondary function of the system was to provide an information service for look up of patient results, both current and previous. The provision of this latter function would obviate the need for a manual filing system. These aims, especially in the way in which they relate to the day to day management of a haematology department, differ quite markedly from the 'total' computerisation concept where every detail of the patient report is computer generated and the process is usually overseen by a large multi-user system.

Figure 5.1 outlines the initial phases of development of the system. With the upgrading of the System 3, patient data could be reviewed, but the problem of convenient access to the data arose since the System 3 had to function as a work

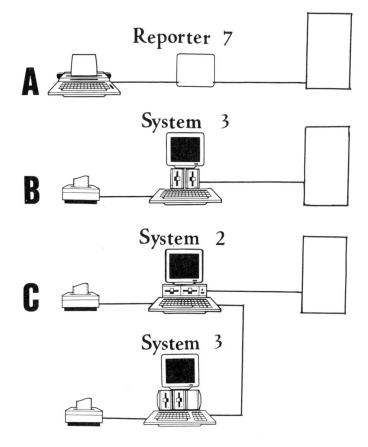

Figure 5.1 First set of development phases of system

station for the updating of patient identification and off-line results, and also provide an access point for patient enquiries.

5.3 Roles of the System 2 and System 3 microcomputers

At this stage, the System 3 undertook a variety of data processing functions. Coulter profile data which had been acquired by the System 2 micro was transferred via RS232 link using BASIC at 9600 baud to the System 3. A minimal degree of 'token passing' was used so that each system could determine which aspect of the data transfer sequence was being undertaken. Each profile was sent once, repeated, compared and if necessary transferred again, though this latter process seems never to have been required. In order to initiate the transfer, the respective menu options in each system were selected and the processes ran in each system with no user interaction.

The System 3 was used to enter patient identification details and results of off-line tests. A Televideo VDU operating at 19200 baud with a 10×14 dot matrix character array was used as the input device. This relatively high quality display minimised problems of eye strain and operator fatigue and was considered an important feature of the overall operation of the system.

Data held on the 5.5 Mbyte Winchester disk was structured into files each containing 6000 records. This file size corresponds to about six weeks' workload, and ensures that copies of data files can be conveniently backed up onto the eight inch floppy drives.

Specimens are processed with reference to laboratory numbers which each year range between 1 and about 60 000. Whilst such a numbering system provides convenient identification for the processing of samples, the establishment of a suitable index is necessary for rapid access to results of selected patients. The main index file on the current data file on the System 3 is updated using 'SUPERSORT' at the end of each day's laboratory processing; this produces an index in order of name, date of birth and laboratory number. The process takes about eight minutes per day operating on a full data disk.

Up to four data files can be accommodated on the System 3 Winchester disk. Records in the two most recent of these files exist in order of laboratory number and can be readily updated. Entries in the two earlier files are physically sorted in order of name, date of birth and laboratory number in order to improve speed of recall of consecutive patient results.

5.4 Cromemco development environment

Software development was undertaken using Cromemco structured BASIC — an advanced implementation of BASIC close to the design of the structured versions developed at Dartmouth College in the late 1970's. This implementation allows a library of program modules to be configured on disk, and provides structured logical constructions such as REPEAT, WHILE and IF THEN ELSE. Flexible methods of manipulation of string variables provide powerful ways of updating the data, particularly patient identification and off-line results. The data structure requires that in the manner of reserving space for numeric arrays, space also has to be reserved for string variables. For example the statement

$$DIM \ T\$(100)$$

reserves 101 consecutive bytes (0 to 100) for the variable T\$. With the string variable area uniquely defined, no form of 'garbage collection' is necessary during program execution. The length of string arrays is limited only by available memory size.

The operating system used in the Cromemco systems is CDOS which, while compatible with CP/M — 80, provides various enhancements such as an 'Ignore Retry Continue' facility (after the fashion now provided by MSDOS) when disk errors are encountered. This facility ensures that the notorious CP/M error "BDOS error in ----" does not force a halt to system operation.

5.5 Implementation of Torch network

The need for the provision of improved access to the accumulating data led to the implementation of the current system configuration (*figure 5.2*), where routine

31

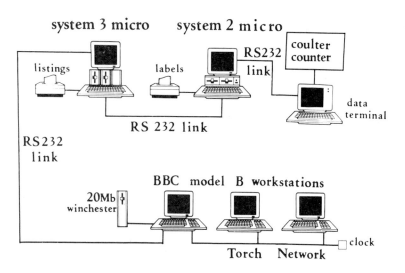

Figure 5.2 Current system configuration

patient enquiries are handled by a Torch network incorporating a 20 Mbyte Winchester disk. The network solution allows the haematologist in the department to have access to the data via a separate workstation. In addition, other functions such as coagulation file updating have been implemented on the network. The initial transfer of complete data files was undertaken using the commercially available 'BSTAM' program using an RS 232 link at 9600 baud. At the end of each working day, a scratch file of up to 200 new results is created on the System 3 and subsequently transferred to the Torch network using BSTAM after which the corresponding index file on the network is updated, again using SUPERSORT. This transfer process ensures that data resides in two independent systems, and so provides an additional level of backup of data.

Up to nine data files can be accommodated on the Torch network Winchester, providing access to just over a full year's worth of data. The two most recent of these files are in the conventional order of laboratory number, whilst the remaining files are physically sorted in order of name, date of birth and laboratory number.

5.6 Torch network environment

Microsoft BASIC, running under the CPN operating system of Torch Z-80 cards, was used to develop facilities for looking up patient data. It was not considered necessary to provide facilities for updating individual records held on the network since these facilities already existed on the System 3.

The Torch network is effectively an extension of the BBC Econet system with a more highly developed software interface. It operates by allowing users to share resources, though mechanisms for establishing such linkage facilities can be relatively complex. Although the 20 Mbyte Winchester is attached to one network unit, it does not act as the default file server of the system. For the purposes of file management, each of its five disk surfaces is defined in terms of logical drives B.C.D. E and F.

Each station can be identified by a network identifier between 1 and 254.

Identifier values of 200 and above can be assigned to so-called privileged stations. Initially the PERMIT function must be used on a given station to allow other stations access to it. Thus 'PERMIT B' would give every other station permission to link to the particular station's drive B for read-only access.

Subsequently a station could use the ATTACH facility to gain access to drive B on the station that had issued a PERMIT directive. The command

ATTACH B to 50 A

would allow drive B to gain access to drive A at station 50. The sequence of PERMIT attachments is established when the station with the hard disk is booted and an autoboot sub file is run. When subsequent stations are switched on, a process is activated to run batch files present on drive B of the Winchester disk relevant to the station being powered up. This in turn ATTACHes the relevant stations to the logical drives of the WINCHESTER disk. The FORBID command can be used to prevent attachment to a station's selected drives and DETACH to cancel previously ATTACHed stations. Once the series of batch files is established, however, the process of access on the network is transparent to users.

5.7 Discussion

The provision of such an information system has proved of benefit in its principal role of accessing current haematology patient profiles. Since most in-patients have haematology tests the data also represent a convenient marker of hospital inpatient attendances. In this role, data have been of use in identifying patients developing post operative wound infections who are referred from community sources without any indication of recent hospital contact.

The availability of networks therefore offers considerable potential for information capturing, processing and sharing, though they need not be directly involved at the 'sharp end' of data capture as in the case of the haematology

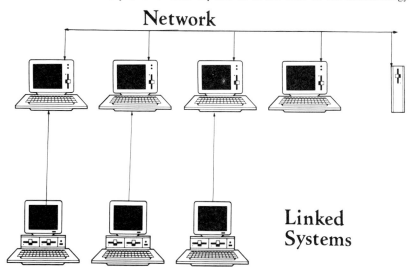

Figure 5.3 The generalised concept of a network providing a 'sink' for data from diverse linked computer systems.

laboratory. In particular, they lend themselves quite naturally to the accumulation of patient profiles after the fashion of *figure 5.3* where data from diverse computer systems can be collected by a centralised network facility. Whilst the problems of interconnection may seem a drawback, the difficulties can usually be overcome, resulting in the development of a system with a high degree of resilience — an important factor for the morale and confidence of the staff operating the systems.

The major limitation to the development of such reporting systems is the quality of the data, especially that of patient identification details. In the experience of the haematology exercise approximately ten per cent of such details have some major or minor error, usually in the accuracy of the date of birth. Patients can appear on different days with different names or the change can come hourly. This represents extra work in trying to sort out the confusion.

Thus network developments can be seen in the light that technology can usually be found to do what is necessary for passing data around, but that difficulties will still remain due to the problems arising out of quality of the data transferred to them.

Reference

1   Gee K C E 1983 *An introduction to local area computer networks* (Macmillan. London)

CHAPTER 6

A Glimpse at the ACR-NEMA Digital Imaging and Communications Standard

P C Jackson
Department of Medical Physics, Bristol General Hospital

6.1 Introduction

There is an increasing proliferation of digital equipment within medical establishments that is both acquiring and archiving patient related information. The management of these systems is coming under close scrutiny with regard to confidentiality[1], but at the same time the medical professions are requiring greater access by electronic means to all patient data acquired on different systems. The objective of many clinicians is to have all data (e.g. images, biochemical assays or clinical records) either stored centrally or available within a network of distributed stations, so that they can be viewed, simultaneously if necessary, at many different locations. A prime requirement in the development of integrating patient data is that the information should be transferred with high fidelity and that additions can be made to the network easily and without corrupting the flow of data.

The uncertainties associated with commercial viability, continued development, and the maintenance of a competitive market make it desirable to formulate a standard whereby equipment can be interfaced in a multivendor environment. Such a standard should allow a modular approach to building an information network without necessarily being constrained to a single manufacturer, or being concerned with the fidelity of data transfer between equipment of different manufacture. In the USA the American College of Radiologists (ACR) and the National Electrical Manufacturers Association (NEMA) have produced a standard method of transferring images (and other image related information) between imaging equipment of different manufacture, from which it should be possible for other data from different sources to be integrated into the system. This standard is based on the ISO-OSI model[2] and is likely to be adopted by most manufacturers of imaging equipment.

The implementation of the standard may have consequences not only for the clinical management of patients but also with regard to the underlying costs of health care. It is conceivable that the electronic availability of information and the use of such a standard may become very important if clinical costing of patient investigations is to become more widespread. For example, a 'clinical costings management system' would access the network to obtain the nature of biochemical investigation performed, the number and type of imaging studies completed, contrast agents used, number of views etc, and hence derive financial transfers between departments. Although the ACR-NEMA standard has not been devised for this specific purpose, clinical costing of imaging procedures is likely to be a very important feature of information networks.

6.2 An outline of the ACR-NEMA standard

The intention of the ACR-NEMA standard on digital imaging and communications[3] is not to provide a network, magnetic tape or picture archiving and communications system (PACS) standard. It has, however, areas of endeavour which seek to promote the communication of digital image information irrespective of source format and equipment manufacturer, whilst also encouraging the development and expansion of PACS that are capable of interfacing with other systems of information. The standard also allows for the creation of diagnostic information data bases that can be examined by a host of devices distributed geographically. In overall concept, the standard restricts the presentation of image data to a known format, although once in the network or within the scope of the equipment the image data may be handled in whichever way is appropriate for the manufacturer or user.

The ACR-NEMA standard is intended to provide a common interface for all types of imaging device, whether connected into a network (*figure 6.1*) or simply between two discrete units (*figure 6.2*)

The ACR-NEMA standard does not interfere with the choice of topology for the network, either 'star', 'ring' or 'bus' (*figure 6.3*), but acts merely as an image conditioning unit prior to data being transmitted or received within the network. In addition to the ACR-NEMA format, a second interface unit is required, known as a Network Interface Unit (NIU), which allows the conversion of image data and information from the ACR-NEMA interface into a format compatible with the network.

The standard specifies a hardware interface for which there is a set of software commands and data formats for image transfer and receipt. In providing this standard, all imaging equipment complying with the requirements will be compatible and able to transfer data. However the mechanisms for validating that

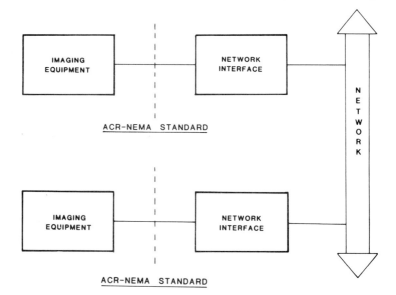

Figure 6.1 An example whereby the ACR-NEMA standard interface would 'condition' the image prior to the network interface unit (NIU) allowing the image data to enter the network and be extracted by another NIU. The data would then be reconverted into an image by the ACR-NEMA format.

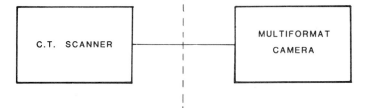

ACR-NEMA STANDARD

Figure 6.2 The ACR-NEMA standard will provide a direct digital link between two items of equipment irrespective of whether there is a network present.

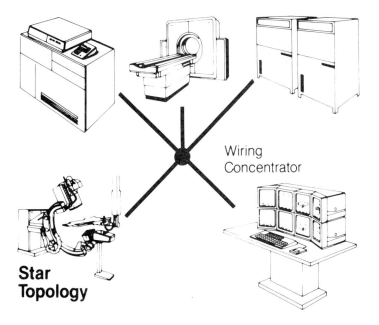

Star Topology

Wiring Concentrator

Figure 6.3 Irrespective of whether the network is configured in a (a) 'star', (b) 'ring' or (c) 'bus' topology, the ACR-NEMA standard will still be applicable. (courtesy of Siemens Medical Systems).

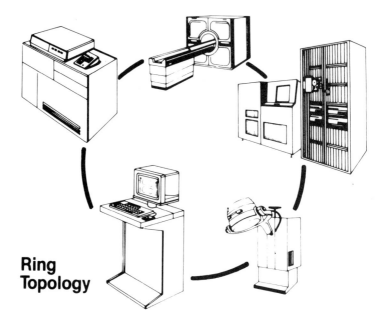

Ring Topology

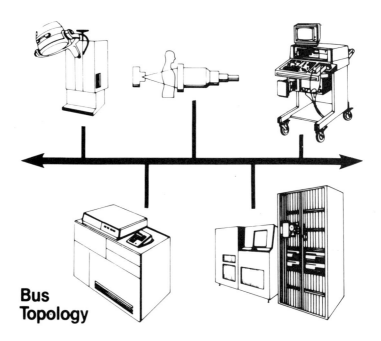

Bus Topology

Figure 6.3 (contd.)

38

manufacturers have complied with the standard have yet to be formulated. It is assumed that the standard will evolve to meet demand, and that early versions of the standard will be fully compatible with further developed systems and will be fully supported by an ACR-NEMA committee. The document describing the standard is organised into ten sections with numerous appendices and it is the purpose of the following section to highlight a few important features of the standard.

6.3 An overview of the ACR-NEMA standard

6.3.1 Hardware and performance

The principal hardware describes a 50-way, microtype connector that can support 16 data circuits, parity line and 6 control circuits (*figure 6.4*). All data is transferred as parallel 16 bit words with parity, along differential pair lines to ease ground and noise problems. The error rates on the 17 parallel lines should be less than 17×10^{-9}. The data exchange is asynchronous so that all types of device can be supported and a physical lower transfer rate of 2 Mbyte s^{-1} is possible although the target rate is 8 Mbyte s^{-1} over any length of cable. However, in the draft version of the standard the specification for cable length was 15 m.

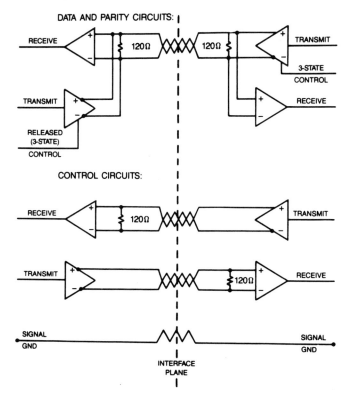

Figure 6.4 The data and control lines are formed as differential pair lines into a 50 way connector. (courtesy of NEMA).

All devices associated with imaging can be classed as an 'image source', 'image sink', 'image source/sink' or 'neither' (*table 6.1*), and all devices have equal standing in that there is no 'master-slave' relation. A device complying with the ACR-NEMA standard must respond to all commands specified in the standard relevant to its function. A valid response to a command which cannot be implemented is 'REFUSED'. For instance, if a CT console sent a command to get an image from a multiformat camera then the response from the unit will be 'REFUSED' because the task is impossible. Those devices that act as an imaging source must be able to initiate a SEND-REQUEST and be able to receive a SEND-RESPONSE. Likewise an imaging sink must be able to receive a SEND-REQUEST and initiate a SEND-RESPONSE. Apart from the ECHO-(REQUEST and RESPONSE) which is mandatory, all other commands and 'handshaking' controls are optional.

The timing of data transfer is important. When a device is requesting to send out data, a minimum waiting time of 1.25 μs and a minimum set up time for data transfer of 70 μs is specified. If the procedure for data transfer between devices has been developed and no transfer occurs between devices within one second, an 'inactivity time out' is instituted and the lines reset. This facility avoids inefficient use of data transfer lines between devices. Since the data lines are bidirectional, data collisions can occur, whereupon the device detecting a collision must delay any further attempt of transfer for a random time of 0 to 15 μs or, if fixed, a minimum time of 7.5 μs.

Table 6.1 Imaging equipment can be defined into groups depending upon whether they are primarily an image 'source', 'sink' or a combination of both

	Image Source	Image Sink	Image Source/Sink	Neither
Archive Unit			✓	
X-Ray CT Unit	✓		✓	
MRI Unit	✓		✓	
DSA Unit	✓		✓	
Ultrasound	✓			
Thermography Unit	✓			
Gamma Camera	✓			
Digital Radiography	✓			
Workstation		✓	✓	
Multiformat Camera		✓		
Printer		✓		
Management System				✓

6.3.2 Operation

The ACR-NEMA standard has a layered structure, similar to the ISO-OSI model of communication (see Chapter 1, section 1.2), having both physical and virtual links between corresponding layers in devices. The standard applies rigorously to all horizontal links between layers, but the implementation of data and control between layers within a device (i.e. vertically) is left to the manufacturer (*figure 6.5*).

The standard specifies five layers; physical, data link, transport/network, session and higher function. Each layer is self contained and data transferred

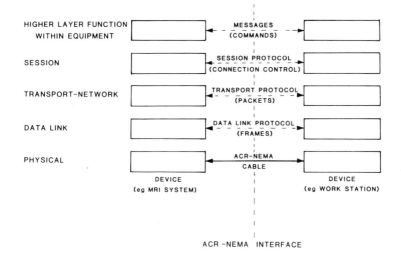

HIGHER LAYER FUNCTION WITHIN EQUIPMENT — MESSAGES (COMMANDS)

SESSION — SESSION PROTOCOL (CONNECTION CONTROL)

TRANSPORT-NETWORK — TRANSPORT PROTOCOL (PACKETS)

DATA LINK — DATA LINK PROTOCOL (FRAMES)

PHYSICAL — ACR-NEMA CABLE

DEVICE (eg MRI SYSTEM)

DEVICE (eg WORK STATION)

ACR-NEMA INTERFACE

Figure 6.5 The ACR-NEMA standard consists of five layers which are either connected physically (solid line) or by a virtual link (dotted lines). All data transferred horizontally have to comply with the standard, whereas the method of vertical transfer within the equipment is at the discretion of the manufacturer.

between layers is well defined. The data is 'boxed' and 'wrapped' into one or more packets depending upon size, and the various wrappings are used to assist other devices in selecting appropriate action, identification of data type, control the flow of data, error checking, etc. Each layer can both add a wrapping to data being sent and remove a wrapping from data being received. The physical layer provides the high speed data transmission used by the data link layer, which in turn 'frames' data from the transport/network layer with control words. The prime purpose of the transport/network layer is to fragment 'messages', which contain data and commands, into blocks of 2048 words. These 'packets' contain sequencing and descriptive headers since each message can contain only one image. The session layer is an interface for the higher function layer which is primarily concerned with application and message format.

In more detail the image data is contained in a message that has both format and content. Each message is organised into groups and all groups are formatted in the same way and appear only once in a message. There is a minimum amount of information required of 'standard' groups, although other groups can be specified such as 'shadow', 'user' and 'manufacturer specific'. There are data set types (i.e. Image, Text, Graphics, Other, Identifier, Null) which are implicitly identified and defined by the groups they contain. For instance 'Other' may contain spectroscopic data associated with an MRI image, and if this was for restricted access it may be put into a 'shadow' group called 'Private Other'.

The message content contains a single data set (e.g. Image) which is arranged and identified by a hierarchical structure (e.g. study, series, acquisition, image) that allows one image to be associated with another. The orientation of image relative to patient and equipment co-ordinate frame is essential (*figure 6.6*) and special display features must be conveyed by lookup tables and linear transformations.

41

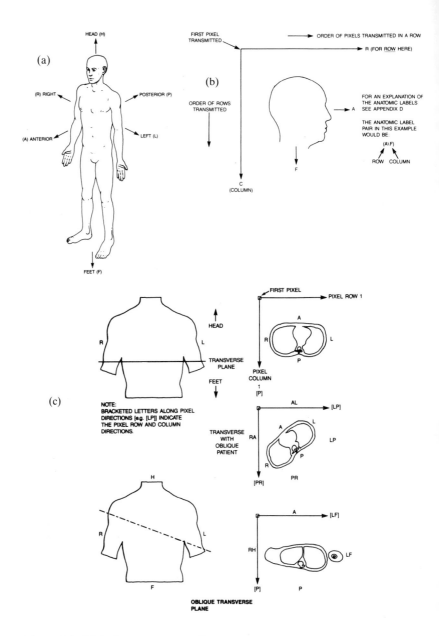

Figure 6.6 (a) An important aspect of image transfer is to obtain the correct orientation of data with respect to the patient. (b) The data are transferred as rows and columns with the row taking precedence in specification. (c) In the top example the data are transferred going across towards (L) and down towards (P), therefore the view is denoted LP. In the complex example of a transverse section in an oblique position the data are transferred going across towards (L) and (P), and down towards (P) and (R). (courtesy of NEMA).

Images are divided into three types; original, modified and composite. The original and modified versions are supported by ACR-NEMA standard, but composite images have to identified by 'Private Group'. In this context, a modified image relates to adjustments in pixel values from the original single image data, whereas composite refers to pixel values which have been modified by the combining of two or more images. For instance, it should be easy to transfer original data from a digital fluorography system or nuclear medicine data processor, but more difficult to transfer a 'subtracted' or 'integrated' image which has been formed from two or more images. This lack of support for composite images may be inconvenient, and no doubt will be rectified in the future.

With respect to overlays and graphics the overlay plane is assigned one bit. Regions of interest (ROI) are treated separately and information related to ROI area, mean and standard deviation of ROI content are also transmitted.

6.3.3 Implementation

The implementation and success of this standard is likely to reside with manufacturers and users who insist on purchasing equipment with this interface facility. If the ACR-NEMA interface is promoted as a standard interface, analogous to the expectations of purchasers with regard to interfaces for disk drives, printers, monitors, etc, then it is likely that it will be quickly adopted into the integrated imaging department. This presupposes, of course, that users wish to transfer images. Such an interfacing standard, being flexible in design, does allow departments and hospitals to gradually build image and data transfers into development programmes without the commitment of a large single capital outlay. Retrospective design and incorporation of the interface is likely to be expensive and probably not satisfactory. The cost of the interface in absolute terms may be more expensive depending on the versatility of the equipment (i.e. whether image source, sink, source/sink, neither), but in relative terms will be inexpensive for the more powerful image data processors. It is likely that within the next two years most manufacturesrs of multi-imaging techniques will offer this facility.

6.4 Conclusions

It is important for the user to support the concepts of such a standard since it allows multivendor purchases and better use of imaging resources. At the present time the standard has been designed around the concepts of transferring basic image data, but the future may require that composite image data be incorporated into the standard. Greater attention in eliminating redundant image information prior to transfer may be required, thus improving the packaging process.

References

1   H M Government UK 1984 *Data Protection Act* (HMSO, London)
2   International Organisation for Standardisation 1983 *InformationProcessing Systems — Open Systems Interconnection — Basic Reference Model* ISO 7498–1983 (International Organisation for Standardisation, 1 Rue de Varembe, Geneva, Switzerland)
3   National Electrical Manufacturers Association 1985 *Digital Imaging and Communications* ACR-NEMA Standards publication No 300-1985 (National Electrical Manufacturers Association, 2101L Street, NW, Washington DC, 20037, USA)

CHAPTER 7

Image Distribution Networks for Nuclear Medicine

P Vernon
IGE Medical Systems Ltd

7.1 Abstract

As computers have been widely used in nuclear medicine for many years now, and many hospitals have more than one such computer, there is a need for an efficient transmission of images from one system to another, and for diagnostic consoles with access to more than one imaging system. The growth of CT and NMR imaging will produce a need for similar systems covering a wider range of image types. Nuclear medicine is an attractive area for development because both technical and medical staff are already used to computers and digital image display systems.

General Electric have been investigating networks for the distribution of all the different medical images. Two networks have been developed for use in nuclear medicine departments, a simple and inexpensive one for hospitals with one to three gamma cameras, and a more sophisticated network for larger hospitals. Key design considerations included high speed, low cost, and conformance with hardware and software standards. These factors are very important for networks and must function in many different hospitals and with equipment of several manufacturers.

The design of these networks will be described, together with explanations of the choices which had to be made. The impact of cost, speed, and organisation decisions on systems for nuclear medicine and for more general imaging networks for radiology and general hospital distribution will be discussed.

CHAPTER 8

Kermit, a Universal File Transfer Protocol?

A R Davies
Department of Medical Physics, Princess Margaret Hospital, Swindon

8.1 Introduction

The rapid increase in the number and variety of computers in use in hospital departments over recent years has brought the benefits of increased efficiency through the availability of more up-to-date and detailed management information, wordprocessors and improved methods of information storage and retrieval. Along with these benefits have come a multitude of problems and irritations: perhaps a major one has been the lack of a standard method of transferring programs and data between dissimilar computers. A variation of this problem was encountered by the staff of Columbia University Centre for Computing Activities, when they became unable to allocate adequate disk storage space on their DEC and IBM mainframes to their large number of students. Their solution to the problem was to devise a file transfer protocol which would enable the transfer of files between their mainframes and a large number of different microcomputers, in order to take advantage of the inexpensive floppy disk storage provided by the microcomputers. The first implementation of the protocol ran on their DEC mainframe and was known as **KL**-10 **E**rror free **R**eciprocal **M**icro **I**nterchange over **T**TY lines, or more usually as **Kermit**. KL-10 is the designation of the CPU of the DEC mainframe. In order that the protocol should be as widely implementable as possible, the RS232 asynchronous serial telecommunications line is employed as the data transfer medium. While some manufacturers deviate somewhat from the defined standard, an RS232 port of some kind is available on the vast majority of all computers, and the fundamentals of RS232C[1], defining the physical and electrical requirements, ASCII ANSI X3.4 1977[2], defining character encoding and ANSI X3.15 1976[3,4], defining the bit transmission sequence, can be supported by these computers. The use of an RS232 line also facilitates the use of modems for transmission of data over dial-up telephone lines and for direct or 'null modem' connections between computers. The primary function of the file transfer protocol is to ensure that the data requested by one computer is transferred via the communication medium to the requesting computer, without the introduction of errors in the data. Errors in the data can be introduced in one of two main ways:

1. Electrical noise or interference in the communication link. This is a particular problem if the two machines are separated by long distances or if a dial up telephone line is employed in the link.
2. Lack of synchronisation between the transmitting and receiving computers. The data must not be transmitted at a rate greater than the receiving machine can process it, otherwise data will be lost.

8.2 Kermit's data structures

Kermit employs the commonly adopted approach for file transfer between computers, in requiring that cooperating programs must run on the two machines involved in the transfer. The sending program divides the outgoing data into discrete packets having a well defined format, illustrated in *figure 8.1*. Each of the fields contains only ASCII characters, and holds the following information.

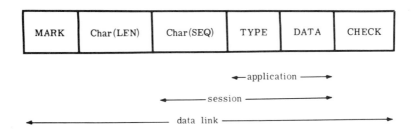

Figure 8.1 Kermit data packet format.

MARK   The MARK field indicates the start of a KERMIT packet. This usually takes the form of the SOH character (ASCII 1).

LEN   A single character defining the total length of the packet. LEN equals the total packet length in ASCII character minus 2, and takes a value in the range 0 to 94. The maximum packet length is therefore 96 characters.

SEQ   A single character indicating the packet sequence number. It is incremented for each new packet which is sent, but on reaching 64 'wraps-round' to 0.

TYPE   A single printable ASCII character describing the type of information contained within the DATA field.

   D — Data
   Y — Acknowledge
   N — Negative Acknowledge
   S — Send Initiate
   R — Receive Initiate
   G — Generic command indicating that the data field holds a single command character followed by any required parameters. Amongst these are commands to request directory listings from the remote machine, to delete files on the remote machine and to display the contents of files held on the remote machine on the local display console.
   C — Indicates that the data field holds an ASCII string representing a system specific command to be executed by the remote computer.
   X — Indicates that the following packets will hold data that is to be displayed on the local console.
   S — Send Initiate
   R — Receive Initiate
   F — File Header
   E — Error
   B — Break Transmission
   Z — End of File

DATA   The information to be carried by the packet. Non-printable ASCII characters are converted into a printable form by adding 64 to their ASCII value and are prefixed with a quoting character to enable decoding by the receiving computer. Similarly, characters with the eighth bit set may be converted to a printable form by subtracting 128 from its ASCII value and again identifying it with a prefix character.

CHECK   A one, two or three character checksum calculated from each of the characters in the packet, excluding the MARK and CHECK fields.

For machines that are unable to accept single character input from their serial input line, a line terminator (usually a carriage return, ASCII 13) can be appended to the packet. Line terminators are not, however, required by the protocol and do not form part of the packet.

8.3   File transfer initialisation data fields

Two further data structures, central to the operation of the Kermit protocol, which contribute to the flexibility of the system are the send-init data field and the corresponding receive-init data field. When a file transfer is requested the source computer sends a packet containing the send-init data, while the receiving computer responds with the receive-init data. In the following description of the send-init data structure, the receive-init data field holds the corresponding information from the receiving machine unless otherwise stated.

MAXL   The maximum length of the packet that the sending machine wishes to be sent.

TIME   The length of time, in seconds, the sending machine should be allowed before being 'timed out'. If an expected packet is not received within this time, a negative acknowledge should be sent by the receiving computer to request the re-transmission of the last packet.

NPAD   The number of padding characters to be sent between packets. These characters may be required by half duplex systems to provide sufficient time for the direction of transmission to be changed.

PADC   The padding to be used. The character is encoded into a printable form. NUL (ASCII 0) is most frequently used.

EOL   The line terminator character to be used if one is required.

QCTL   The printable ASCII character to be used to quote control characters and prefix characters.

QBIN   The printable ASCII character to be used to quote characters that have the eighth bit set. Used for transmitting binary files when either system is unable to use the parity bit for data.

CHKT   The number of characters to be used for the checksum, either '1', '2' or '3'. If the send and receive CHKT fields do not agree the system defaults to a single character checksum.

REPT   The character to be used to prefix a repeated character. Usually a '~'. If the send and receive REPT fields are not the same, then repeated character coding will not be used.

CAPAS   Used to identify any special facilities available, such as file attribute packets, etc.

A further four fields are reserved for future use, and individual implementations of the protocol make use of additional fields beyond these for their own purposes.

8.4 Basic Kermit commands

1. SEND and RECEIVE

These are the two most fundamental commands in any Kermit implementation. The SEND command has the following syntax:-

SEND file_specifier

where file_specifier is a single filename or defines a group of files using 'wild card' characters (usually '*') to match with any character or string of characters.

RECEIVE is the complementary command to SEND and is issued to the receiving computer.

The state diagram of *figure 8.2* illustrates the process involved in transmitting a file or group of files between two computers operating the Kermit protocol. The key to Kermit's ability to transfer data reliably lies in the fact that every packet that is sent should result in an acknowledgement from the receiving machine. If the packet has arrived and the error detection system has found no error, a packet acknowledging the receipt of the good data is sent to the source machine. If, however, an error is detected in the received data, or an expected packet does not arrive within a set period of time, a negative acknowledge packet is sent to the source machine, prompting it to re-send the lost or corrupted packet.

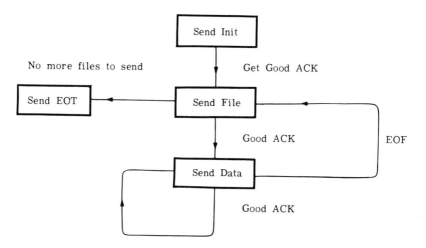

Figure 8.2   State diagram of source machine for a Kermit file transfer.

2. CONNECT   This command puts the local machine into terminal emulation mode, and establishes a link with the remote computer.

3. SET   Allows a variety of system parameters to be initialised including:

BAUD-RATE
PARITY
RETRY   The number of times to send a given packet before aborting the transmission.

BLOCK CHECK	The number of characters to be used for error checking.
PORT	Sets the communications port to be used on computers with multiple ports.
SEND	Allows the user to set each of the fields of the send-init field to values other than their default.
RECEIVE	Set receive-init parameters.
4. EXIT	Causes the kermit program to stop and returns the user to the operating system.

Most implementations of Kermit also support a context sensitive 'help' facility, which lists all possible options available at a given time. Entering '?' at the Kermit prompt would cause all of the basic Kermit commands to be displayed, while entering 'SET?' would list each of the parameters that can be altered by the SET command.

8.5   Kermit in use

A typical Kermit session, to transfer a set of files from a mainframe computer to a microcomputer might be conducted on the microcomputer as follows:

A>	: micro operating system prompt
A>kermit	: Run Kermit on the micro
kermit-80>	: Micro Kermit prompt
kermit-80>connect	: Connect to mainframe in terminal
	: emulation mode

[Connecting to host. Type CTRL-]C to return to PC]

Mainframe login message	: connection to mainframe established
@ login	: Log into system
@ kermit	: Run Kermit on mainframe
Kermit-20>	: Mainframe Kermit prompt
Kermit-20>send∗.pas	: Send all Pascal sources files

CTRL-]C	: Escape sequence to return to micro

Kermit-80>receive	: Instruct local Kermit to
	: accept files from mainframe

(Details of the packets successfully transferred are written to the console)

[Transfer Complete]

Kermit-80>connect	: Return to mainframe

[Connecting to host. Type CTRL-]C to return to PC]

Kermit-20>exit	: Leave mainframe Kermit
@ logout	: and log out of remote system
[logout message]	

CTRL-]C	: Escape back to micro

Kermit-80>exit	: Leave micro Kermit
A>	: Back to micro operating system

In this example Kermit-80 is running on the local microcomputer, and Kermit-20 on the remote mainframe. Messages from the Kermits are in square brackets.

8.6 Conclusion

The procedures adopted by the Kermit protocol ensure that files can be readily transmitted even over poor quality data links. Kermit has been implemented on well over one hundred different computers, from a version for the Commodore 64 written in Forth to one for the Cray-XMP written in Fortran-77. The more recent implementations of the protocol have many more advanced features than those described in this paper, including the option for one machine to act as a file server to another, taking all its commands from Kermit packets. The full range of features available using the Kermit protocol is described in the Kermit User Guide[5] and the Kermit Protocol Manual[6]. The main centre for the distribution of Kermit file transfer programs in the UK is: The Computer Centre, University of Lancaster, Bailrigg, LANCASTER LA1 4YW.

Acknowledgements

'Kermit' is a registered trademark of Henson Associates, Inc. The Kermit protocol was designed at the University of Columbia Centre for Computing Activity by Bill Catchings and Frank da Cruz. Free distribution of programs based on the protocol is encouraged by its designers, although the protocol is subject to copyright.

References

1   EIA 69 Standard RS-232-C 1969 *Interface Between Data Terminal Equipment and Data Communication Equipment Employing Serial Binary Data Interchange* (Electronic Industries Association, 2001 Eye Street N.W., Washington D.C. 20006, USA)
2   American National Standards Institute 1977 *Code for Information Interchange* Publication ANSI X3.4-1977 (American National Standards Institute, 1430 Broadway, New York 10018, USA)
3   American National Standards Institute 1976 *Bit Sequencing of ASCII in Serial by Bit Data Transmission* Publication ANSI X3.15-1976 (American National Standards Institute, 1430 Broadway, New York 10018, USA)
4   American National Standards Institute 1976 *Character Structure and Character Parity Sence for Serial by Bit Data Transmission* Publication ANSI X3.16-1976 (American National Standards Institute, 1430 Broadway, New York 10018, USA)
5   da Cruz F 1984 *Kermit User Guide* (Columbia University Centre for Computing Activities, New York 10027, USA)
6   da Cruz F 1984 *Kermit Protocol Manual* (Columbia University Centre for Computing Activities, New York 10027, USA)

Discussion on Networks

The main item of discussion at the end of the first day's session was the practicality and cost of implementing the ACR-NEMA standard. It was pointed out that at present this was a costly exercise, as the image data has first to be converted from the format used by a particular machine (e.g. CT Scanner) to the NEMA format by using a computer. A further interface was then required to connect the NEMA signal to a network such as Ethernet. It was emphasised that the ACR-NEMA standard was not an overall network standard for the transmission of images.

It was stated that the cost of Ethernet hardware was approximately £1500 per node. This figure did not include software costs or manufacturer's profit.

It was established that it takes about one hour to transmit a 1.5 Mbyte image using JANET. This time may be reduced in the near future as faster methods of data transmission such as 'Kilostream' are used. It was thus apparent that image transfer using JANET was best suited to 'one-off' rather than routine applications.

50

CHAPTER 9

Methods of Digital Image Processing used by the National Remote Sensing Centre

C Legg
National Remote Sensing Centre

9.1   Introduction

Some of the methods used by the National Remote Sensing Centre to process images obtained from Earth-orbiting satellites will be discussed. The images that will be considered were acquired by the TIROS-7 satellite, which operates at an altitude of 1000 km. Each pixel of the image is equivalent to an area of at least 1.1 km^2 and the data is acquired at five wavelengths, one approximating to visible red, another to the near infrared and three in the thermal infrared. *Figure 9.1** is a colour composite image of a part of Morocco produced by superimposing three wavelength bands to give an approximation of true colour. *Figures 9.2 to 9.4** show the effects of processing on the original image.

Processing allows enhancement of the images, to emphasise features of interest, examination of correlations between different data sets and automated classification and recognition of areas of images with similar characteristics.

9.2   Processing single-band images

Single-band images are those produced by a single wavelength of radiation. A range of processing techniques can be used to enhance and classify these images.

9.2.1   Contrast stretching

In many digital images the range of digital values (the dynamic range of the image) is rather small, and the image therefore lacks contrast. Contrast stretching will distribute the digital values over the full range (0 to 255 for an 8-bit system) of the display system, resulting in increased contrast. *Figure 9.2* shows a monochrome near-infrared image overlaid by histograms of pixel values before and after a Gaussian contrast stretch.

9.2.2   Image rectification

There may be defects in the digital image due to sensor malfunction, geometric distortion or simply missing information. These can be rectified on most image processing systems by using de-striping, geometric correction and other algorithms.

9.2.3   Density slicing

The human eye can perceive differences of colour with much greater sensitivity than it can differences in grey tones, and it is often advantageous to assign colours to specified ranges of digital numbers in order to enhance the image. This process

*Figures 9.1 to 9.4 appear on the back cover of this report.

is known as density slicing. The process can either assign a single colour to each specified range or merge one colour with the next, the latter technique preserving more detail of the original image. *Figure 9.3* shows a density sliced version of the infrared image shown in *figure 9.2*.

9.2.4 Smoothing

Various smoothing algorithms are available, most of them based on a moving average box filter. These are used to generalise the original image and thus emphasise large scale features.

9.2.5 Linear filters

It is often useful to extract information on linear features within an image which may be obscured by surface detail. Linear filtering techniques pass a gradient filter over the image in a specified direction in order to emphasise selected directions of linear features.

9.3 Processing multiband images

Multiband images can be composed of broadly similar data sets (for example a scene or an object viewed in different wavelengths of light), or may combine totally different data sets of the same area or feature (for example temperature, magnetic field strength and copper distribution). Most image display systems operate with three colour guns, as in a colour television, so that only three data sets can be displayed simultaneously, using the blue, green and red guns.

9.3.1 Colour composites

The simplest method of combining three data sets is to display them as a colour composite image, with each data set allocated to one colour gun of the display. Each single-band image is contrast-stretched so as to present the maximum information in the resulting colour composite. *Figure 9.1* is an illustration of this technique.

9.3.2 Differences and ratios

It is often possible to extract additional information from images by comparing the digital numbers between different channels of data. This can be done by subtracting one from the other, to obtain a difference image; dividing one by the other, to obtain a ratio image; or by a combination of mathematical operations. Apart from highlighting specific features of interest, these processes can have the effect of condensing the data, reducing a large number of original data sets into three composite data sets which can be displayed as a single colour composite image.

9.3.3 Principal components

There are a range of mathematical techniques for extracting the main features of multicomponent data-sets. The one most used in image processing is principal components analysis. As the name implies, this process extracts the principal components (principal axes) of ellipsoids containing digital numbers of the various data sets in multidimensional space. There are as many principal components as there are data sets, with the level of significance of the components decreasing from first to last. The principal components can be displayed as single band images, or in the form of colour composites, and have been found to be a very effective form of data compression.

9.3.4 Classification

It is often necessary to extrapolate from a known portion of a digital image to a larger unknown portion. A specific feature, or group of features, might have been identified in one portion of an image, and information might then be required about the distribution of these features over the whole image. This can be done semi-automatically by a variety of classification processes. In most of them a training area, or group of training areas, is defined from known data. The image processor then calculates the average and range of digital numbers for the training area, and searches the rest of the image for values lying within the same range. In the case of multiple training areas, statistical maximum likelihood techniques can be applied to assign pixels to one class or to another. *Figure 9.4* shows a five class maximum likelihood classification of the original multiband image. The colours represent the following surface cover types: red - cultivated area, green — grassland, dark blue — rock upland, yellow — thorn scrub, light blue — sand desert.

Other classification techniques may recognise textural or pattern information in the data and classify accordingly.

CHAPTER 10

Holographic Displays of Medical Data

J Drinkwater* and S Hart
Blackett Laboratory, Imperial College, London

10.1 Introduction

Several medical imaging techniques, such as X-ray CT, MRI and PET and several analytical techniques, such as electron microscopy, yield data from a sample volume. Current tomographic systems present a set of planar images and do not fully exploit the possibility of complete three-dimensional imaging. Holographic techniques[1] can combine a set of two-dimensional cross sections to provide a three-dimensional visualization of the sample volume in a hologram. Such a display is potentially a valuable addition to the detailed information on each slice shown by conventional displays, providing a better understanding of the spatial relationships between material in different images. Holography could form the primary three-dimensional display or act as a hard-copy medium to supplement other systems. The techniques could be useful for diagnosis, treatment planning, patient monitoring and archiving of medical data, as well as having wide applications in other areas of science and engineering.

Multiple exposure or volumetrically multiplexed holography has been investigated for the display of tomographic data. Radiologists routinely obtain cross sections through the human body representing parallel two-dimensional slices through a volume. These cross sections can be simultaneously displayed by sequentially recording a hologram of each cross section in the same holographic emulsion. The resulting hologram has both vertical and horizontal parallax and produces a full set of three-dimensional depth cues for an observer. Transmission holograms have been produced for viewing on a novel white light display device based on dispersion compensation[2]. This device provides a convenient high quality display that can be used in ordinary lighting conditions.

10.2 Techniques

A multiplexed hologram incorporates many holograms of separate two-dimensional images. The human visual system naturally perceives a scene as being three-dimensional if these multiple two-dimensional images are appropriately presented.

Holographic multiplexing falls into two categories:

1. **Lateral**, in which a series of two-dimensional views are obtained each showing the whole data from a separate perspective view. A series of thin strip holograms are then made, each showing one of these views. This produces a 'stereogram' in which each eye sees a different perspective thus producing a three-dimensional image by stereopsis. This technique loses one direction of parallax but gives a hidden line capability[3,4].

* now with Racal Research Limited, Reading RG2 0SB.

54

2. **Volumetric**, in which a series of two-dimensional cross-sections through the data are sequentially exposed at different distances from a holographic emulsion. The resulting 'stack' hologram possesses both horizontal and vertical parallax, and the details of the back slices can be seen through the front slices as though the object was totally transparent.

Volumetric multiple exposure holography has several advantages over other potential techniques for the display of medical data:

1. Tomographic data is routinely obtained as parallel cross sections through a volume. Such data is almost immediately suitable as input for multiple exposure holography after a small amount of pre-processing.
2. The holograms provide a full set of depth cues for an observer, who can focus onto each individual plane in the displayed object.
3. The hologram is an additive display, the eye seeing a volume of data as the sum of light emitted from each image point. This reduces the amount of obscuration compared with other (non-holographic) techniques where structure in one plane can be obscured by information in planes towards the front of an image[5].

10.3 Procedure for production and display of holograms

10.3.1 Data pre-processing

Volumetric multiplexing requires an input in the form of a set of two-dimensional slices through a volume. Medical tomography data is thus well suited to this technique after minor image pre-processing. Generally the only processing required is the selection of a suitable grey scale window to aid perception of the final three-dimensional image. The amount of information presented in a hologram has to be limited to prevent confusion from the detail in each slice, and to reduce obscuration of the rear slices by information in the front of an image. In general unwanted information, such as large areas of uniform density repeated from slice to slice, is supressed, whilst desired information is highighted. For example, in neurological scans the grey matter is generally supressed to reduce obscuration whilst features of interest, such as bone, tumours, blood vessels and reference points (e.g. the ventricles) are retained or enhanced. It is also important that successive slices are in the correct lateral positions as proper registration is important for the perception of continuity and spatial relationships between material in successive slices.

10.3.2 Production of a hologram

A white light viewable multiple exposure hologram is generated by a two step process. In the first stage, a 'master' or H1 hologram is produced. Each individual cross section is projected onto a diffusing screen with light from a helium-neon laser. The diffused object wave propagates to the recording plane where it interferes with an off-axis reference wave from the same laser. The interference pattern is recorded on 200 x 250 mm holographic film or plate (Agfa Gevaert 8E75HD). After each exposure the diffuser is translated with respect to the recording plane and the next cross section displayed. The net result is a multiple exposure hologram where the cross sections are imaged at a depth in the display corresponding to the position from which the data was originally obtained. This sequence is shown in *figure 10.1*.

Typically holograms of approximately 20–30 slices can be superimposed in the

(a) Recording geometry

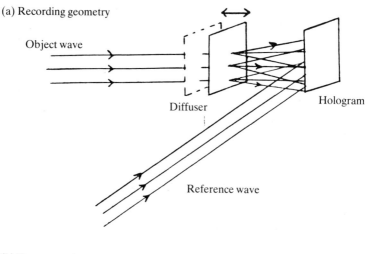

Object wave

Diffuser

Hologram

Reference wave

(b) Reconstruction geometry

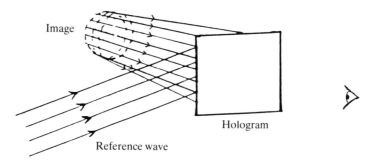

Image

Hologram

Reference wave

Figure 10.1 (a) Hologram recording (production).
(b) Hologram reconstruction (display).

same emulsion with a good signal to noise ratio. It should be possible to increase this figure in the future, the current limit being set by available data. The trends in hologram efficiency and signal to noise ratios can be derived from scaling arguments. If N holograms are recorded in one emulsion then the fringe modulation available to each is reduced by a factor $1/N$ compared to a single exposure. Then the radiance of any one of the reconstructed wavefronts is about $1/N^2$ of the radiance of a single image stored in the same emulsion[6]. Scattered noise from the hologram depends only on the total exposure and the area illuminated. So the signal to noise ratio of any one image varies as $1/N^2$, while the signal to noise for the composite image varies as $1/N$. The limit to the number of slices that can be displayed will be set by signal to noise considerations, determined by the emulsion, the processing and the input data.

The second stage involves making a 'transfer' or H2 hologram from the original H1. After development the H1 hologram is illuminated with the conjugate of its original reference wave so that a real 1:1 magnified image is formed. This image is used as the object for the production of a second hologram, by introducing a second off-axis reference beam and recording the interference pattern in a second holographic plate. After processing, the H2 hologram formed can be considerably brighter than the H1 (approximately a factor N) and image planed (i.e. the plane of the hologram emulsion passes through the centre of the image), making it suitable for white light display. The holograms produced are 200 x 250 mm in size with a usable image volume of approximately 150 x 150 x 150 mm.

10.3.3   Display of hologram

For holographic techniques to be of general utility it is essential to display the final holograms conveniently in ordinary lighting conditions. Image plane transmission holograms have been produced specifically for display on a novel viewing device based on dispersion compensation. The technique retains high image luminance and full (both vertical and horizontal) parallax. An auxilliary diffraction grating is used to produce an equal but opposite chromatic dispersion to the hologram, so compensating (to a first order approximation) the transverse chromatic aberration in the image[7]. The optical elements required have been combined in a compact self contained unit of screen size 280 x 280 mm and depth 300 mm. When a transmission hologram made at the correct reference angle is placed on the unit an achromatic (black, white and shades of grey) image is reconstructed. The holograms are back-lit giving the twin advantages of a high tolerance to ambient lighting without reconstructing spurious images and ease of detailed examination of the images. This display technique enables the final holograms to be viewed with high brightness and clarity in ordinary room lighting.

10.4   Results

Holographic techniques have been applied to the display of data from several areas in medicine, biology, science and engineering. In medicine data from techniques such as MRI (e.g. cardiology), X-ray CT (e.g. neurosurgery) and electron miscroscopy (e.g. pathology) have been used. The optical hardware and computer software have been implemented, enabling a hologram to be synthesised from a general data set. The work has demonstrated that high quality, high brightness displays with good signal to noise ratios can be produced to provide a better understanding of spatial relationships within the information.

Several techniques with potential value for medical interpretation and records have been demonstrated. The optical stages introduce no distortions so that dimensions on the final hologram relate exactly 1:1 to the input data. Thus it should be possible to make unambiguous measurements from the images. It is also possible to superimpose two or more holograms on a viewer which will reconstruct simultaneously. The overlay of images should allow comparisons between images. For example, data obtained by different imaging modalities or at different times could be overlaid for rapid and easy comparison.

10.5   Potential applications

Holographic display techniques can be applied to any area of science or medicine that has a requirement for the display, interpretation, communication and storage of three-dimensional information. A hologram could act as a hard-copy for three-dimensional data in much the same way as conventional film routinely produces hard-copy of two-dimensional data. The methods are well suited for the display of medical data as medical imaging techniques routinely obtain cross sections through the human body and there is a requirement for the display and interpretation of this data. Applications envisaged are in areas such as diagnosis, surgery planning, and radiation therapy. A detailed knowledge of the spatial relationships between structures is crucial in areas like neurosurgery, where a surgeon could need to remove a biopsy sample from the correct position without touching any blood vessels, or in radiation therapy where it is important to match the volume irradiated to the tumour and to minimize damage to healthy tissue.

10.6 Conclusion

This work has demonstrated the potential of holography for the display of three-dimensional data. High quality, high brightness holograms have been produced from medical imaging data with relatively little pre-processing. The laboratory exposure system has been automated and it would be feasible to integrate the whole system into an automated unit requiring a skill level equivalent to a conventional X-ray unit. Many imaging techniques inherently deal with volumetric data and initial reactions indicate that holographic displays will aid in the presentation, communication and interpretation of such data.

Holography could be used as a primary form of three-dimensional display in conjunction with conventional two-dimensional displays to provide an alternative and supplementary view of the data. Equally holography could be used as a form of 'hard-copy' enabling simple presentation, transfer and storage of patient records. Holography could also provide a three-dimensional hard copy capability for the sophisticated computer systems of the future, in much the same way as conventional film is used today. Hence it is envisaged that holographic displays will be widely used in the future.

Acknowledgements

We are indebted to Kaveh Bazargan, Chris Dainty, Michael Dalton and Francis Tuffy for advice on optics and image processing, and to the hospitals and individuals who have permitted us to process their data. This work was supported by the Science and Engineering Research Council.

References

1 Collier R J, Burckhardt L H and Lin L H 1971 *Optical holography* (Academic Press, New York)
2 Bazargan K 1985 A practical, portable system for white light display of transmission holograms using dispersion compensation *Proc SPIE* **523** 24
3 Debitto D J 1969 Holographic panoramic stereograms synthesised from white light recordings *Applied Optics* **8** 1740
4 Newswanger C and Outwater C 1985 Large format holographic stereograms and their applications *Proc SPIE* **523** 26
5 Hesselink L, Johnson K M and Perlmutter R L 1983 Holographic display devices *Proc SPIE* **402** 36
6 Caulfield H J 1970 Wavefront multiplexing by holography *Applied Optics* **9** 1218
7 Burkhardt C B 1966 Display of holograms in white light *Bell Systems Technical Journal* **45** 1841

CHAPTER 11

Problems in the Preparation of CT Images for use in Radiotherapy Treatment Planning

G S Shentall and J A Brace
Medical Physics Department, The Royal Free Hospital, London

11.1 Introduction

Radiotherapy aims to give a known dose of radiation to an anatomically defined region of a patient, usually for the treatment of cancer. Traditionally the area to be treated has been planned in a single plane using x-ray films to determine the position and size of the target. However, the advent of computerised tomography (CT) scanners has now made it possible to take multiple slices through a region of interest and to define a target with a three dimensional shape. This paper looks at some of the problems involved in the preparation of CT images for three dimensional treatment planning.

11.2 Overview of procedures

Once a patient has been scanned the image slices obtained have to be prepared for treatment planning. It is quite normal for the treatment planning to take place at a site separate from the CT scanner, so arrangements have to be made for the data to be transferred. Direct data links between the CT scanner and the treatment planning system are not always possible and data is often transferred by floppy disc or magnetic tape. In our case the data is recorded onto 256 kbyte single density floppy discs by a Siemens scanner, with 14 slices on each disc.

The next stage is to enter this data into a Philips Oncology Support System (OSS). First of all a conversion program is run which converts the Siemens scans into the format recognised by the Philips CT viewing software. The resulting data are then stored on a 1 Mbyte floppy disc, which holds a maximum of 36 slices. Individual planes are then chosen by the clinician and entered into a routine called 'Prepare RTP' (i.e. Prepare Radiotherapy Planning) in which the patient's body outline and any other features (e.g. the target area or critical structures) are drawn and superimposed onto the CT image. After storage on another floppy disc, editing of the patient details, and modification of the outlines, the prepared scans are saved on a final floppy disc and are considered ready for planning. The maximum number of CT planes with outlines stored on one floppy disc of this type is 14.

The way in which the planning proceeds from this point depends upon the type and complexity of the treatment envisaged by the clinician. In most cases the dose distribution is calculated on the Philips OSS with two to four radiation beams being directed at a single isocentric point in the centre of the target. If, however, a more complex treatment is desired (e.g. using a moving isocentre), then the treatment has to be planned on our own Hewlett Packard (HP) mini-computer system.

A Midas micro-computer has been programmed to act as a peripheral device under the control of the HP computer to read data from the Philips OSS discs. Data transfer between the HP mini-computer and the Midas micro-computer is achieved using a 16 bit parallel interface. The HP system can hold up to 50 CT slices on the system disc and uses magnetic tape for long term data storage. All 50 slices can be used to provide a projection of the target volume from any angle. Using these projections a treatment plan is devised and a file created containing the intended movements of the treatment machine. This file is then transferred to an HP micro-computer in the radiotherapy department via a hardwire link. The treatment is given by a TEM MS90 cobalt unit under the software control of the HP micro-computer using the machine movements held in the patient's individual treatment file[1,2].

Inherent problems associated with some of the above stages in the preparation of a treatment plan will now be looked at in more detail.

11.3 Coordinate systems

To treat the target in a spatially precise manner an accurate coordinate translation must be made between the position of the patient in the CT scanner and the position of the patient during treatment. It is important, therefore, to set up a patient coordinate system that is both well defined and reproducible.

A reference patient coordinate system is first of all established in the CT scanning room. Lasers with special optics are used to project two perpendicular planes onto the patient's skin; one vertical and one horizontal, with the planes intersecting along the axis of rotation of the CT scanner. These are then marked onto the patient and the distance of the horizontal plane above the couch is noted; this is called the lateral reference height. Thin radio-opaque markers are taped along the reference lines of the patient so that the coordinate system will be visible on the CT scans. Longitudinal alignment is achieved by marking onto the patient's skin one or more CT plane positions as shown by the scanner indicator light[2].

Once the patient coordinate system has been defined it is not an easy matter to impose this onto the CT image. Theoretically it is just a matter of aligning a set of axes with the radio-opaque markers seen on the CT image, but practice has shown that patients tend to relax during the scanning session so that the lateral markers no longer form a horizontal plane with a consistent reference height from slice to slice. If this is the case, then the reference height position is averaged from the lateral markers on all the slices.

Putting this into practice has also presented problems because the Philips OSS does not readily lend itself to this kind of patient coordinate system. Instead it uses an anatomical reference point (actually a small closed contour) which is drawn using a light pen onto one of the CT slices displayed on the monitor screen. This point cannot be positioned at the origin of the two reference planes with any degree of accuracy, so an origin displacement correction is measured from the centre of the CT scans and applied by the HP mini-computer when the Philips data is read into the system. Once the coordinate system is established in this way, an isocentre position inside the patient can be defined uniquely using absolute treatment couch positions.

If a patient is to be treated under computer control, then a treatment file is prepared on the HP mini-computer and transferred to the micro-computer in the radiotherapy department. The file consists of a set of instructions designed to move the treatment machine automatically after the patient has been set up by the radiographers. Three lasers similar to those in the CT scanning room are used to line up the reference marks drawn onto the patient's skin so that good alignment of the patient is achieved at the start of each treatment, although some variation in patient positioning exists from day to day. Therefore, although the treatment file is prepared using absolute machine control parameters, the computer will read the position of the treatment couch at the start of each treatment and will use these positions as the basis for all its translational movements for that particular treatment. The computer software will also warn the operator if the start position is unsatisfactory. For example, a collision situation may be detected, or there may be a problem with the patient's position on the couch, with insufficient machine movement left in a particular direction to complete the treatment.

11.4   Outline drawing

A necessary stage in the preparation of a CT scan image for treatment planning is that various outlines be superimposed upon it. These outlines serve several purposes both to the physicist planning the treatment and to the computer: they clearly show all the clinically important features of the scan (e.g. the target area and any sensitive structures); they aid the computer dose calculations by precisely defining the body outline; and they are used for printing hardcopies on XY-plotters and standard printers.

When a particular scan is selected for planning the computer will automatically attempt to draw in the body outline. This is usually done by a contour following algorithm which first of all searches for a point with a particular Hounsfield value (about half way between the values for air and water) by interpolating between pixels, and then follows a contour of points with an equal value. Although this method normally works well there are some inherent problems associated with it. An operator will always have to confirm that the computer operation was correct because it is never certain that what has been outlined is the patient's body. An example of this is that the Philips OSS computer often outlines and labels one of our reference markers as the body outline. Another problem is that a special low density couch top is needed so that the algorithm will not confuse the couch with the patient. In our case this means placing a thin piece of hard foam beneath the patient because the method usually fails with the normal wooden couch top (which has a Hounsfield value of about –550).

All other outlines are drawn by the operator using a cursor on the TV monitor. The cursor position can be controlled by a variety of devices including a light pen, digitizer, tracker ball and scratch pad. There are advantages and disadvantages to each of these devices with no ideal winner. A light pen is quick and simple to use but suffers because it is not always stable and it is difficult to see the anatomy on the CT scan beneath the large highlighted cursor. The other devices are more stable but practice is needed in controlling the cursor position because of the translation the operator needs to make between movement of the device and the resulting movement of the cursor.

11.5   Conclusion

It will always take time to produce the data needed to reconstruct a realistic model of the patient and target volume in three dimensions. At present, using the Philips OSS, it takes the clinician most of a day to convert the Siemens data, analyse the individual CT scans and draw on all of the necessary outlines. The major benefit of doing this is being able to devise a treatment that matches the shape of the target more closely and reduces the volume of tissue irradiated to a high dose[3].

References

1 Brace J A, Davy T J, Skeggs D B L and Williams H S 1981 Conformation therapy at the Royal Free Hospital: a progress report on the Tracking Cobalt Project *British Journal of Radiology* **54** 1068–1074

2 Davy T J 1985 Physical aspects of conformation therapy using computer controlled tracking units, in *Progress in Medical Radiation Physics* (ed C G Orton) **2** 63–73 (Plenum Press, New York)

3 Tate T, Brace J A, Morgan H and Skeggs D B L 1986 Conformation therapy: a method of improving the tumour treatment volume ratio *Clinical Radiology* **37** 267–271

Practical Experience of Image Transfer from Nuclear Medicine, X-ray CT and Video Sources to a VAX Computer

A J Britten, A C Keen, J S Fleming and P J Howlett
Wessex Regional Department of Medical Physics, Southampton General Hospital and St. Mary's Hospital Portsmouth

12.1 Introduction

We report our experience of image transfer from medical imaging systems to DEC VAX 11/730 computers with Sigma 7000 display processors operated by physicists from the Wessex Regional Medical Physics Department. There are two VAX 11/730 and Sigma 7000 systems, situated in Southampton General Hospital and St. Mary's Hospital Portmouth, which form part of a programme to develop a general medical image handling facility. The image processing software is an in-house developed Fortran package (PICS) and this report describes the transfer of images to the VAX and their storage in a common format for subsequent processing.

We shall use the terms 'hub computer' to describe the system receiving the images (VAX 11/730) and 'satellite computer' to describe the system sending the images.

Table 12.1 shows the systems transferring data to the hub VAX and the transfer method used. With only a limited budget the choice of data transfer method was largely determined by the existing hardware available.

Table 12.1 Summary of systems and methods used.

Satellite system	Transfer method	Hub (VAX) software required	Satellite system software required
Link Maps 2000	Magnetic tape	User Fortran program	Link disk-to-tape copy program
Link Maps 2000	Serial line	Link DECLINK and user Fortran program	Link DECLINK
MDS A²	Magnetic tape	User Fortran program	MDS disk-to-tape copy program
IGE Star	Magnetic tape	DMR Computer Ltd. User Fortran program	IGE disk-to-tape copy program
Picker 1200SX	Magnetic tape	User Fortran program	Picker disk-to-tape copy program
Siemens Somatom DR2	Floppy disk	DEC VMS Exchange User Fortran program	Siemens floppy-to-hard disk copy

12.2 Hardware

12.2.1 Magnetic tape

The Medical Data Systems (MDS) A², IGE Star and Picker 1200SX systems use magnetic tape as their removable storage medium. The VAX has a Cipher F880 microstreamer tape drive capable of handling 9 track phase encoded tapes at a data density of 1600 bpi (bits per inch) on up to ten inch diameter reels. The IGE Star and Picker 1200SX tapes were written in the same mode whereas the MDS A^2 tapes were written in 9 track NRZ (Non Return to Zero) at 800 bpi. An intermediate copy step was therefore carried out on the Southampton University ICL 2976 mainframe with a tape-to-tape copy utility copying the tapes to the correct format.

The Link Maps 2000 systems originally had Lark 16 Mbyte cartridge disks as its only removable media. The cost of buying a similar drive and controller for the VAX was considered prohibitive so the use of magnetic tape was selected, after a period of use of serial line data transfer (see 12.2.3). Since the Link tape was to be used for the daily transfer of limited amounts of data, usually less that 5Mbytes per day, a compact tape drive capable of using 900 feet tapes was purchased (EMI 9800 Streamer) and the coupler installed into one of the Link Maps 2000 systems. This provides 17 Mbytes of unformatted data capacity on one seven inch reel.

12.2.2 Floppy disks

The Siemens Somatom DR2 whole body scanner has a DEC PDP-11/24 system with 8¼ inch double sided double density floppy disks as its removable storage medium. A DEC RX02 dual floppy disk drive and controller was purchased and installed on the VAX. Each disk can store up to six 256 x 256 images, three per side, in uncompressed data mode.

12.2.3 Serial line

A serial I/O board (Link Systems DECLINK) was installed in one of the Link Maps 2000 systems. This board allows serial transmission or reception of data at up to 9600 baud in asynchronous mode using the XON/XOFF protocol. The line at the VAX end was connected to one of the six available serial input/output ports with no additional VAX hardware required.

12.2.4 Video signal capture

Two distinct types of devices may be considered for video signal digitisation. The first device is physically situated in the VAX/Sigma system, either plugged into the VAX Unibus or into the Sigma 7000 display processor bus. The second type of device is a separate portable system capable of digitising and recording an image for subsequent transfer to the VAX as digital information over a parallel data line. The latter device is more flexible since it may be moved to different locations to record the video signal, with the main drawback being the greater expense due to the need for a fast Winchester disk sub-system to record the captured image. The image capture rate for the portable system will be faster than that of the integrated system because of the dedicated disk drive and the single task optimization of the system. In view of the hardware cost advantage a system resident in the VAX/ Sigma system was chosen, and in the absence of an existing product for the VAX 11/730 Unibus, a custom built device has been developed by Oggitronics electronics in conjunction with Sigmex.

12.3   Reformatting the images

12.3.1 Information required to read the images

The first step in attempting image transfer is to approach the manufacturers of the system with a request for information about the data formats and file storage. The companies we have dealt with have proved to be extremely cooperative and have freely given full information and help. This cooperation has been given with only the obvious requirement of non-disclosure of detailed information to third parties.

As with most tasks, the easiest solution is to find someone who has done it before. If such a person can be found it may prove simpler to modify their programs than to start from scratch; we have followed this principle in adapting the Royal Marsden's program for IGE Star to VAX transfers. We have received invaluable help from a variety of sources who are gratefully acknowledged at the end of this paper.

When considering a transfer process we need to know the following details:

1. Physical medium characteristics
    A summary of the details required is given in *table 12.2*. These details are essential to determine whether one can physically access the data.

Table 12.2   Physical medium characteristics.

Medium/Transfer method	Details required
Magnetic tape	Reel size. Number of tracks. Encoding mode: Phase Encoded (PE) or Non-Return to Zero (NRZ). Data density (bpi).
Floppy disk	Size. Data density (single/double) Tracks per inch (tpi). Hard or Soft sectored.
Serial line	Signal standard (eg RS-232). Baud rate. Synchronous or Asynchronous. Communication protocol (Number of bits, parity, start/stop bits).
Video	Interface bus.

2. Operating system details
    The name and version number of the operating system must be known. Different operating systems and manufacturers have different file and media directory structures. Knowing the details of each system (the hub and satellite systems) one is able to determine whether a file written under one operating system can be accessed under the other; commercial software may be available to carry out this task.

3. File location
    We need to know how to find a given image file on the medium. On disk the file will usually be found by the operating system using the disk directory; the user need only know the file name. Disks written by a different OS may need to be read by a utility program to cope with the different directory and file structures. For example, we use the DEC Exchange utility to convert files written to floppy by the DEC RT-11 operating system to the DEC VAX VMS operating system format.
    Finding files on magnetic tape is in principle much simpler than the corresponding problem on disk because of the sequential nature of tape storage. Knowing details of the tape labelling and the sequence of files on tape will enable us to access any tape file required.

4. File format

Having found the file we need to know what each byte in the file represents. This information must be supplied by the manufacturer, or by a third party with the manufacturer's consent.

12.3.2 Reformatting the data

The process of converting the image from the satellite to hub system file and image format is referred to here as reformatting. This procedure depends upon how the data on the removable medium may be accessed. The first case is one in which data can be read directly from the medium under the user's program control; the data is read, reformatted and written to another storage device. If, however, the medium cannot be read directly by the user's program then a utility program must be invoked to copy the files from the removable medium to hard disk in the correct format. This latter procedure is necessary for the VAX to be able to read files written onto floppy disk by the Siemens Somatom DR2 PDP 11/24, and this is carried out using the DEC Exchange utility which copies data from the floppy disks to the hard disk in the correct VAX format. These VAX files are then read by the Fortran reformatting program and an image file in the hub system image file format created. If the latter procedure needs to be followed we see that the amount of hard disk space required is approximately twice that used when reformatting directly from the removable media, since there must be sufficient space for both unreformatted and reformatted data. This may be an important consideration when copying large amounts of data.

12.4 Local software

Armed with the above information, the local software may now be designed. The software may be viewed as four segments

1. finding the correct image file
2. reading the image file
3. converting the image to the hub system image format (reformatting)
4. saving the image on disk.

Before embarking upon details of this design we have found it invaluable to first examine the raw data in the file. This may help to clear up any ambiguities in the available documentation by allowing us to compare actual and expected data formats. It may also show more fundamental differences in data storage; for example, comparing the storage of two byte words on both Perkin Elmer 11/32 and Data General NOVA systems to DEC systems, the high and low bytes are reversed. This fact may readily be seen by inspecting a printout of the bytes of data in the image file, and we therefore recommend that either a system utility is used (for example DEC Dump on the VAX) or that a simple utility program is written to read a file and print the byte data.

As in many other applications, the use of modular software is encouraged. Amongst other benefits is the fact that subroutines written for one transfer process may be easily used for a subsequent transfer task, and may also be easily modified for use by another user.

Normal data backup procedures have been used on the satellite systems to write data to the removable media. Commercially written programs have also been used to control the transfer of data across the serial line (Link DECLINK) and to read files from the IGE Star magnetic tapes (MDR Computer Ltd.). These programs carry out the task of receiving or reading data from the satellite system and presenting it to the user's program for reformatting.

12.5 Additional features

12.5.1 Directories

The listing of all physical files on a disk will usually be available as a system command. A list associating patient details with each file name may be obtained either by reading a patient file directory, if such a file exists on disk, or by reading each physical image file and determining the patient details from the data within the file. We have not found directory listings for images on floppy disks to be necessary due to the small number of images stored on each disk (up to six). Directory listings of files on magnetic tape are, however, essential due to the potentially large number of files on the tape. The Picker 1200SX and IGE Star tapes have tape file directories which allow us to inspect and select files after reading and decoding the directory file. The A^2 tapes do not have a file directory on tape and so a directory is created by reading all files on the tape and storing the essential patient details and file numbers in a disk file for reference.

12.5.2 Error recovery

Intermittent tape hardware errors during writing of the MDS A^2 has resulted in some data corruption on tape. This is particularly serious since this data is recorded in a compressed mode and thus image position within a file cannot be predicted. Error recovery procedures have been implemented, with limited success.

12.6 Performance

We have used two transfer times as approximate indicators of the performance of each transfer path (*table 12.3*). The first indicator is the reformatting time, defined here as the time taken to read and reformat an image, with the timing started as the reading of the image file commences. The second indicator is the screen-to-screen time, defined as the average time between identifying an image on the satellite system screen and then viewing the same image on the hub system screen. For comparability these times have been quoted for a 256 x 256 image matrix, with these numbers being estimated for the Link MAPS 2000 and MDS A^2 systems by simple extrapolation from the 64 x 64 matrix tranfer times. Note that these times

Table 12.3 Satellite-to-hub transfer performance for a 256 x 256 image matrix .

Satellite system	Reformatting time (sec)	Screen-to-screen time (min)	No. of keyboards commands
Link Maps 2000 (magnetic tape)	60	3	9
Link Maps 2000 (serial line)	480	8	7
MDS A^2	50	**	7
IGE Star	40	9	7
Picker 1200SX	50	15	10
Siemens Somatom DR2	60	12	11

**Not quoted due to the extra 2 days required for 800bpi NRZ to 1600 bpi PE conversion

are only very approximate estimates as they depend on many randomly varying factors, such as total system usage during the copying procedure.

An estimate of the complexity of the task may be indicated by the total number of keyboard commands issued by the operator. Other factors need to be taken into consideration when evaluating performance, one being the constraint on the rest of the system operation during the data transfer process. This point is particularly important for single user systems which cannot acquire image data during data transfer, or for systems whose overall performance is significantly degraded by the transfer process.

12.7 Summary and discussion

Image transfer paths from five different medical imaging systems to a VAX 11/730 computer have been established. The information required to carry out this task has been obtained from the system manufacturers and from other experienced hospital users. The use of the Southampton University tape copying resources underlines the assistance which a local university may be able to offer. Good cooperation from staff within the imaging departments is essential, and we have enjoyed the cooperation of the staff at local hospitals.

When comparing the relative merits of the transfer methods, factors other than simple image transfer time must be considered; for example the operator time involvement, complexity of operation and the system limitations during tranfer. These considerations have lead us to supercede the serial line data transfer method (Link DECLINK) by magnetic tape data transfer for the transfer of gamma camera data. *Table 12.3* shows that there is a significant time expenditure required to obtain images from several systems. This is primarily a problem of physical location and shows that the time taken to determine which images are required, to arrange a convenient copying time and to actually walk between sites should not be underestimated.

Demand for limited system resources on the hub computer may lead to a significant bottleneck in the transfer process, and we have found this to be so when attempting to service the needs of data transfer, archiving and data retrieval with only one tape drive. The hub system disk space may also be a limiting factor, and we experience frequent space shortage with the VAX 11/730 120 Mbyte hard disk.

We believe that, for our data transfer purposes described here, magnetic tape is superior to floppy disk as a removable medium. This is due to the large data capacity of each tape and the fact that, because the data may be read directly from the tape by the user program, operator intervention is minimal. The main limitation is that file access times are long (up to ten minutes) for files near the end of the tape.

In contrast, floppy disks have low data capacity and fast file access times. The general incompatability of disk formats between manufacturers and operating systems makes disk transfer methods less favourable, since use of a utility program, if available, to convert file formats may require significant operator intervention and greater disk space. If, however, the user program may access data directly from the removable disk then the low data capacity of floppy disks may be their only unattractive feature.

We would stress that we are reporting only what we have found to be appropriate for our situation, and would envisage that other system requirements may be more appropriately met by the use of other transfer processes.

The authors would be pleased to offer any assistance to others travelling along the road to multi-modality imaging!

Acknowledgements

We gratefully acknowledge the help and advice received from the following companies and individuals:-

Mr N Boyce (IGE Ltd.), Dr R Lawson (LINK Systems Ltd.), MDR Computer Ltd., Oggitronics Ltd., Picker Ltd., The Royal Marsden Hospital and Institute of Cancer Research, SIGMEX Ltd., Staff of the Nuclear Medicine departments at Southampton General Hospital and St. Mary's Hospital Portsmouth, and of the Wessex Bodyscanner unit and Wessex Neurological X-ray Centre.

CHAPTER 13

Technical Factors Involved with the Superimposition of Digital Images

E M Pitcher*, P C Jackson, H Key and P H Stevens
*Department of Medical Physics, Southmead Hospital, Westbury on Trym, Bristol and Department of Medical Physics, Bristol General Hospital

13.1 Introduction

At present many Picture Archiving and Communications Systems (PACS) are being developed for all imaging modalities. These afford the potential of displaying and combining related data sets from different imaging techniques in order to improve diagnosis and therapy. Combination of images is likely to be useful when the data sets give complementary information, such as in the case of X-ray computerised tomography (X-ray CT) images, which give anatomical information, and single photon emission computerised tomography (SPECT) images which give functional information.

The aim of the present work was to display and combine X-ray CT and SPECT images and to investigate the problems encountered. In order for image combination to be useful the images must have equal pixel sizes and the image sets must be able to be correctly aligned in both the transverse plane of the patient and along the longitudinal axis. Although the patient will inevitably be the main cause of misalignment it is necessary to test for any systematic, instrumental, differences between the image sets. Phantoms were therefore designed in order to test the scaling and registration of the image sets. The method of transfer of the digital image data is described briefly.

13.2 Materials and methods

13.2.1 Acquisition and transfer of digital image data

Digital image data were acquired on an EMI CT5005 whole body X-ray CT scanner with an independent viewing console based on a Data General Eclipse and on an IGE 400T gamma camera with a Link Systems Maps 2000 image processor. The clinical data used were X-ray CT images of the chest and SPECT images of lung perfusion, as these were being collected as part of a clinical study on acute lung disease.

The image data were transferred between data processors using magnetic tape as a common medium and using a standard format recommended by the American Association of Physicists in Medicine[1]. In this format all descriptive information is stored in a directory at the beginning of the tape and the image sets are stored as multi-dimensional arrays in sequential files. The directory information is in the form of Key-Value pairs such that each Value, e.g. patient name or matrix size, is linked with a descriptive name or Key.

Image data can be transferred in either direction between the two systems; however most of the work on the display and combination of the images was carried out on the nuclear medicine image processor. The transfer of image data is described in more detail elsewhere.[2]

13.2.2   Display and combination of images

In order to display the X-ray CT images on the nuclear medicine system two main problems have to be overcome. Firstly the X-ray CT images, originally collected in a 320 × 320 matrix, have to be packed into a 128 × 128 matrix. This is the maximum practical size for further image processing, although they could be packed into a 256 × 256 matrix for display alone. Secondly the X-ray CT image data has a range from −1000 to +1000 Hounsfield Units (HU). The frame buffer on the nuclear medicine system is only eight bits deep so the dynamic range has to be reduced without, if possible, losing information content. Fast interactive windowing on the nuclear medicine system was not considered feasible so several options were considered.

1.   Simple scaling i.e. linear compression of the dynamic range of CT numbers into the range 0–255. For each image the minimum and the maximum pixel values (H_{min} and H_{max} respectively) are found and each scaled pixel value, S, is calculated using the following equation:

$$S = 255 \ \frac{(H-H_{min})}{(H_{max}-H_{min})}$$

2.   Selective windowing. The maximum and minimum pixel values are assigned according to the chosen window and the equation shown above is used. Scaled pixel values below 0 are set to 0 and those above 255 are set to 255.
3.   Local histogram equalization. The technique used is that described by Pizer[3]. The colour, or grey level, of each pixel is assigned according to the local distribution of pixel values surrounding that pixel. The method is based on the general technique of histogram equalization where a histogram is made of the pixel values in an entire image and the colour levels are assigned so that there are equal numbers of pixels in each level. Local histogram equalization is approximated to by dividing an image into a grid of elements, typically 64 in number, and carrying out histogram equalization for each element. The final colour level of an individual pixel is obtained by bilinear interpolation between the colour values calculated from each of the four nearest grid element centres.

The X-ray CT and SPECT images are combined by superimposing one upon the other using a standard program available on the nuclear medicine system. The frame buffer is eight bits deep which allows two independent four bit colour scales, one for each image. The images shown use a red and a blue scale but other colours may be chosen.

13.2.3   Phantoms

In order for useful information to be gained from the combination the two image sets must have the same pixel size and they must be able to be aligned in both the transverse plane of the patient and along the longitudinal axis. These three factors were tested by the use of two perspex phantoms, one based on a grid and the other on a cone. The phantoms were hollow cylinders of 250 mm internal diameter containing various test objects which could be filled with an aqueous solution of ^{99m}Tc. As the CT numbers of perspex and water differ these phantoms were suitable for imaging on both systems.

The grid phantom (*figures 13.1, 13.2*) was designed to test pixel size and alignment in the transverse plane. Three hollow cylinders, arranged on the circumference of a circle at 120° to each other, tested for translational and

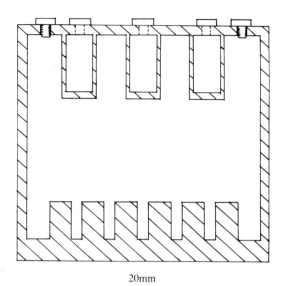

20mm

Figure 13.1 Schematic diagram (sagittal view) of the grid phantom used for detection of translational and rotational movement. The cylinders can be seen at one end and the castellations at the other.

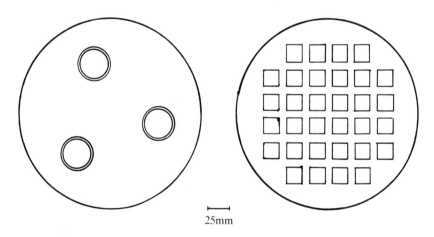

25mm

Figure 13.2 Transverse sections through the grid phantom at either end showing details of the three cylinders and the castellations.

rotational alignment. The castellations (castle battlement-like structures) gave a finer test for alignment and also tested for distortion. This phantom was imaged on both the X-ray CT system and nuclear medicine system in, as near as possible, the same alignment. This was done by using a spirit-level to ensure an engraved line along one end of the phantom was horizontal. The mean internal diameter of the phantom, in pixels, was measured using computer generated profiles across the

72

reconstructed images, and the mean pixel size was calculated by dividing the internal diameter of the phantom (in mm) by the mean number of pixels.

The cone phantom (*figure 13.3*) was designed to test the longitudinal alignment of the image sets. It consisted of a hollow cone with two solid perspex rings at either end which could be identified as markers on both X-ray CT and SPECT images. The distance from the marker of the centre of any slice could be calculated from the diameter of the cone on the reconstructed image. The complete length of the phantom was imaged on both the X-ray CT and the SPECT; the slice thicknesses of which were nominally 12.6 mm and 12 mm respectively. The slice containing the marker was picked out and the diameter of the cone in each succeeding slice was measured using profiles across the reconstructed images for both the X-ray CT and the SPECT image sets.

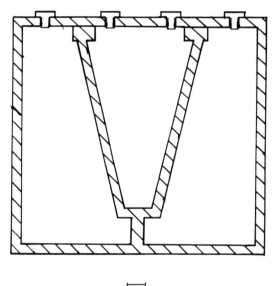

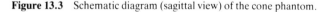
20mm

Figure 13.3   Schematic diagram (sagittal view) of the cone phantom.

13.3   Results

Figure 13.4* shows a typical X-ray CT image of the chest as displayed on the nuclear medicine system using four different display methods. The first image demonstrates simple scaling, the second and third show the effect of selecting different windows and the fourth demonstrates the effect of local histogram equalization. *Figure 13.5** shows the superimposition of an X-ray CT of the chest and a SPECT lung perfusion image. *Figure 13.6** shows the superimposed X-ray CT and SPECT images of the grid phantom. The pixel sizes, for a 128 × 128 matrix, were as follows:

$$X\text{-ray CT pixel size} = 2.98 \pm 0.01 \text{ mm}$$
$$SPECT \text{ pixel size} = 2.97 \pm 0.03 \text{ mm}.$$

* Figures 13.4 to 13.7 appear on the front cover of this report.

The superimposed cylinders showed that the SPECT image was rotated by three degrees relative to the X-ray CT image.

The transverse and longitudinal alignment of the image sets is demonstrated by the superimposition of the images of the cone phantom shown in *figure 13.7**. The distance of the centre of a particular slice from the chosen marker was calculated (as described in section 13.2.3) for both the X-ray CT (D_x) and SPECT (D_s) image sets. The graph in *figure 13.8* shows the actual distances of each slice from the marker in the SPECT images plotted against those for the X-ray CT images. A straight line may be fitted to these points where:

$$D_s = 0.987\,D_x + 0.51$$

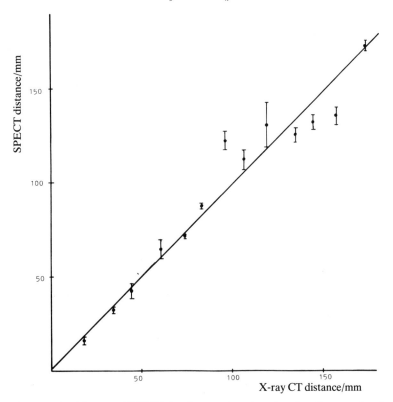

Figure 13.8 Distance of SPECT slice from marker plotted against distance of equivalent slice in the X-ray CT image set. The actual distance of the centre of each slice from the marker was calculated from the measured diameter of the cone and the known dimensions of the phantom.

13.4 Discussion

Combinations of images from different modalities will only be useful if extra information is obtained. The purpose of displaying X-ray CT images on the nuclear medicine system was to provide anatomical information to aid interpretation and quantitation of SPECT images. The X-ray CT images could be displayed on the nuclear medicine system with some loss of resolution and contrast. The resolution loss was due to the packing of the image into a 128 × 128 matrix and was inevitable; however the images obtained were adequate for the intended purpose. The contrast loss was considerable if simple scaling was used to display the image; however if only a narrow range of CT numbers was required then selective windowing increased the contrast in that range. Local histogram equalization appeared to be the best method of increasing the image contrast. The image shown in *figure 13.4d* gives soft tissue and bone detail as well as showing the lung vessels. The disadvantage is that the colour level of any particular pixel loses any physical meaning.

Image sets may be superimposed if the pixel sizes are equal and they are aligned both along the longitudinal axis and in the image plane. Pixel sizes may be matched by simple interpolation of the images based on the ratios of the original pixel sizes. It has been shown that it is possible to align the X-ray CT and SPECT images along the longitudinal axis provided that the slice thicknesses are known and that the image sets contain a marker which is identifiable in both modalities. In the clinical study quoted the sternal notch was chosen as an anatomical marker as it could be clearly identified on the X-ray CT images and also, if a radioactive marker was placed on the sternal notch, on the SPECT images. The results from the cone phantom showed that the slices matched well for the complete image sets and no correction was required.

The three degree rotation of the SPECT images relative to the X-ray CT images, which was demonstrated by the use of the grid phantom, was caused by the reconstruction technique used for the SPECT images. This rotation could be avoided by positioning the camera three degrees from the zero position before starting the acquisition. Alignment in the plane of the image was only attempted after matching of images along the longitudinal axis. In all the studies registration was done by visual means using recognisable features of the phantoms as markers. Although the use of automatic alignment for similar images such as those obtained from lung perfusion and ventilation studies has been suggested by various authors[4,5] this may not be suitable for dissimilar images. Rubber mapping[6] may also be useful although again reference points must be identified for each pair of images.

The work reported in this presentation was concerned specifically with the transfer, display and combination of X-ray CT and SPECT images. The development of PACS allows the possibility of transferring data between systems and many of the problems encountered and the solutions suggested in this paper would be relevant to the combination of digital images from any of the imaging modalities.

References

1 Baxter S B, Hitchner L E and Maguire G Q 1982 *A standard format for digital image exchange* American Association of Physicists in Medicine report no. 10 (American Institute of Physics, New York).
2 Pitcher E M, Stevens P H, Davies E R, Goddard P R and Jackson P C 1985 Transfer and combination of digital image data *British Journal of Radiology* **58** 701–703
3 Pizer S M, Zimmerman J B and Staab E V 1984 Adaptive grey level assignment in CT scan display *Journal of Computer Assisted Tomography* **8** 300–305
4 Appledorn C R, Oppenheim B E and Weltman H N 1980 An automated method for the alignment of image pairs *Journal of Nuclear Medicine* **21** 165–167
5 Barber D C 1982 Automated alignment of radionuclide images *Physics in Medicine and Biology* **27** 387–396

6   Kinsey J H, Vannelli B D, Fontana R S, Miller W E, Johnson S A and Gilbert B K
    1975 Application of digital image detection to diagnosis and follow-up of cancer
    involving the lungs *Application of Optical Instrumentation in Medicine IV* SPIE **70**
    99–112

CHAPTER 14

An Implementation of a Multi-Format Computerised Image Display System

A N R Law and P G B Ross
Department of Biomedical Physics and Bioengineering, University of Aberdeen

14.1 Introduction

In any large hospital there are a number of imaging techniques available to the clinicians. Radiography, X-ray CT and ultrasound are all common and the new techniques of NMR imaging and digital radiography are appearing more widely. Where a number of techniques are available there is a need to be able to make comparisons and this is usually done using some form of photographic reproduction. This is certainly the easiest form in which to store and transport images but when making comparisons there is no possibility of correcting contrast, colour, or size differences. Also, the data from the various techniques cannot be combined in an attempt to extract more information.

As most of these medical imaging techniques are computer based, some form of computerised image display system could be used to allow images from different systems to be viewed under the same conditions. In a sufficiently flexible environment the ability to make direct comparisons and to combine data would be attractive to both clinical and research staff. The successful implementation of such a system requires a computer with image display facilities that is independent of any one imaging technique. In Aberdeen we have such a system which is funded by the Medical Research Council as part of a series of trials into the diagnostic usefulness of NMR compared with other imaging techniques. This system consists of a Digital Equipment Corporation VAX 11/750 computer coupled to Sigmex ARGS 7000 image display hardware. This drives two workstations, one in the department for research use and the other in the hospital for clinical use. As no suitable software was available to control the imaging hardware the design and implementation of a comprehensive package for this purpose was undertaken.

14.2 Design considerations

There are a number of major design criteria in the implementation of the image display system. Of these the most important was to allow for the varied nature of the intended users. In a combined clinical and research department, such as ours, there are two groups of users who have different requirements. The clinical staff require reliable and consistent software giving all the display functions that they may need. Ease of use is important as it is necessary to limit training time and to lower any resistance to using new software. For research staff, although reliability and consistency are important, there is a need for flexibility so that the software can be adapted to their specific needs. Also, by giving the same system to both sets of users, demonstration of new techniques and their future implementation for the clinical staff is greatly simplified.

Ease of use is very important in software packages especially if users are to change from software they have written themselves. To make the change as easy as possible, it is necessary that the system can be tailored to the user's needs, and that extensive on-line information be present on all the functions that are available. Furthermore, all mistakes should be trapped and have understandable explanations with directions on how to correct the mistake where possible.

The system should also provide, as standard, basic tools for the manipulation of the images and for the extraction of quantitative information. The features that we have found to be required include the ability to draw areas and lines of interest, and to display both numerically and graphically the data selected. Scrolling and zooming of images are also needed, as are facilities for manipulating the colour translation tables to give the users full control over the colour scales used to display their images.

To provide the necessary environment for displaying images from more than one source, the system must be designed with the ability to take in data from any type and number of data files. It is also necessary that the display software can treat groups of images, such as an imaging session on a patient, as connected. This allows the user to move forwards and backwards through a series of connected images without having to identify them individually. This also allows for the adoption of an internal naming format consisting of a session identifier, a frame identifier to indicate the data set within a session, and lastly a version identifier to select between different versions of the same image contained in the data set. The session is identified by the user and the frame and version identifiers are numerical values giving the frames and versions in sequence. This format is independent of how the user's data is stored. As the system deals with groups of images it will also be possible to make internal connections betwen image sets from different sources, as will be the case when comparing NMR and radioisotope images from the same patient.

If the display system is to be used by research workers to display data from new processing techniques, it would be useful if processing programs could be easily incorporated into the display system. To this end, the design of the display system includes a simple interface to allow it to be used as a front end to user programs.

The design also takes into consideration a number of other items so that areas of future expansion will not be neglected. For example, we intend to incorporate save and recall features which will allow the user to save a display and all associated information for future recall. Further to this, we hope to provide some ability to program sequences of image displays as an aid to lectures or case conferences. Another area for future incorporation is the display of sequences of images in pseudo real-time such as those produced by gated heart studies in both NMR and radioisotope imaging. Also, the combining of sequences of images to produce three dimensional displays is under investigation and will be added to the display system in due course.

A final consideration in our design was the desire to use the same software to drive imaging hardware other than the main ARGS 7000 system. Display hardware designed and built in our department will be connected to a Microvax II and it is intended that the same software package be used to control this hardware. To this end the image display system is designed around a set of well defined routines which perform all hardware dependent tasks.

An underlying reason for taking this approach to our imaging software is to make the maximum use of the computer system. A single program with most of the desired facilities available will save the time and effort of the computing staff in the continuing education of the users to provide the same features in their own programs. It will also reduce the impact on other resources that results from the multiplication of effort as each user constructs their own imaging software.

14.3   Implementation of design

In the implementation of such an image display system the interface with the user is of major importance. This area of the program is constrained by the limitations of the terminals used. In our case we have used software tools available on our VAX system to construct a user interface that allows command entry from the keyboard, by cursor selection from a menu or by single key entry through function keys. Any of these choices are available to the user and they are free to change between them as they wish. The status of the various components of the imaging system are reported to the user through a series of overlayed displays. The users are also given the facility to construct a file of commands for the system to perform when it is started. This allows the users to tailor many aspects of the system to their own needs.

A more complex part of the implementation is the input of the image data. This data is stored in data files in a number of different formats depending upon the imaging machine that produced it. Other formats are also present as a result of previously written image processing and display programs. One solution would be to convert all data files from other systems to some standard format and then to allow only this format to be used with the image display system. However, with the variety of data file formats already used and the strong pressures against change from resident users, converting to a standard image file format does not offer many advantages. The overheads in both extra processing and storage to support a standard file format are significant, and create extra work for the users which is something we wish to avoid. Instead of a standard file format it was decided to set up a database of file format descriptions into which the user could enter new descriptions as they arise. Each format is given a unique name by the user and this is used to identify data in this format to the display program. The image display program uses the information in this database to find how the image data of a given format is stored and how to interpret the file names. Other information on colour tables and how to process the data can also be stored in the format database if the user requires.

This format database will allow the research users to display their images on the system with the minimum of preparatory effort. To allow for new processing techniques a simple interface between the display program and the user's own routines is provided. This interface allows image data to be transferred to routines written by the user. The data can then be processed and the processed data transferred back to the image display program for display.

A trackerball is available as part of the Sigmex display system and this is used in the image display program to control various display functions such as drawing regions of interest and controlling zoom and scroll.

14.4   Conclusions

It is difficult to produce software packages that please everyone, but to achieve the maximum possible facility for the largest number of users a package such as the one we have described is a good solution. The reduction in duplication of effort is difficult to estimate but from our own knowledge should be significant. With the same program in use both in research and clinical work, transfer of ideas into clinical use will be greatly eased. By removing the barriers that exist between the different imaging techniques, this type of system gives the facilities for comparison between techniques that will be important in the future of medical imaging.

CHAPTER 15

Recognition Applied to Medical Images

J A Newell and E Sokolowska*
*Department of Medical Physics and Biomedical Engineering, Queen Elizabeth Hospital Birmingham and * Department of Computer Science, University of Aston*

15.1 Introduction

The existence of medical images in digital form presents the challenge of processing those images to enable the human observer to obtain more from them. This was done in the past even with analogue images, for example on film. Films were duplicated onto high gamma emulsions to increase the image contrast. The process of unsharp masking was used to enhance edges. Radiographs were taken before and after introduction of contrast material into the blood vessels, one of them then reversed, and the two added to provide effective subtraction leaving only the blood vessels visible.

15.2 Digital processing

All these processes can be achieved that much more easily when the images are in digital form. No film processing is needed, with the time that involves, and no inflexible choice of initial processing conditions is required. All is achieved by software, with very great flexibility, and any degree of non-linearity can be introduced. The main processes can be divided into two distinct classes.

The first class involves alterations of the values of individual picture elements (pixels) without regard to the values of the pixel's neighbours. These processes include contrast enhancement, which can be linear or non-linear, and contouring by pixel value. They also include histogram equalisation, or more general modification, to make better use of all the displayable grey levels. These processes can be performed, effectively instantaneously, with modern digital processing and display equipment. Images can also be subtracted from each other very rapidly and this is used particularly, and very widely now, in the method of Digital Subtraction Angiography (DSA). In this an image, before the introduction of contrast medium into the circulation, is subtracted from an image after the introduction, to obtain an image of the blood vessels alone.

The other distinct class of digital image processing involves the neighbours of a pixel as well. The new value of a pixel is the result of combining the old value together with weighted values of its neighbours. It is a process of convolution. If addition is used, then an averaged or smoothed image is obtained. It acts effectively as a low-pass spatial filter. If differences are used, then a differentiated image is obtained leading to the enhancement of edges or other rapid spatial changes. It is effectively a high-pass spatial filter. The high-pass filters can be given directional preference to enhance edges lying along a particular direction.

These methods of processing all lead to new images. They are used in order to obtain images in which features that are sought will be more easily identified and recognised. But the identification and recognition will remain with the observer. The results of the methods are still images, and the examination of those images is performed in the same way as the examination of the original image.

15.3 Automatic recognition

As a further large step in identification the computer itself can be used to achieve some sort of automatic recognition — to identify known anatomical structures in the image and to select the unusual or the abnormal. The approach that we have adopted is that of structural pattern recognition. To some extent this contrasts with the rather older statistical pattern recognition. In the latter an image is described in terms of statistical features which may be rather far removed from the structure of the image itself. The recognition process then involves comparing the statistical features with features gathered from normal and abnormal images and obtaining some measure of normality or abnormality for the image under consideration. Principal component analysis is an example of that approach. In structural pattern recognition, the actual structure of the original image is retained throughout the recognition process. A symbolic description is obtained of the original image in terms of regions and their properties, such as density value, position, size, shape, and so on. This description, preserving the original structure, is then compared with a similar description, in anatomical terms, of the expected features in the image. Matching takes place, enabling one to label the regions of the original image with anatomical descriptions, or with some measure of abnormality. We have applied this process successfully to CT images of the brain. This general approach has been used in other fields and an interesting example is an elaborate system built for the automatic interpretation of aerial photographs[1].

15.4 Segmentation

The procedure is first to decompose the image into segments corresponding to regions of similar density (pixel value). This is done by the split-and-merge method of Pavlidis[2]. There is a wide choice of condition that can be applied to test a region for uniformity. We have chosen to use the condition that a region is uniform if pixels within it do not depart from the mean value of the pixels in the region by more than a chosen threshold value. The image is split into square blocks which are split further, or merged, resulting in blocks that are uniform and correspond to the nodes of a quartic picture tree. Adjacent blocks are then tested for uniformity, and merged if appropriate, resulting in segments that are uniform and consist of one or more of the blocks. Blocks are described by the coordinates of their top left hand corner and the length of their side, and carry with them characteristics of their pixel values. Segments are described by the numbers of the blocks of which they consist and by a table giving their adjacency to neighbouring segments. Additional features of the segments can be calculated if these will aid the recognition process. These might be description of shape and of texture for instance.

What we now have is a symbolic description of the original image in terms of regions of uniformity with characteristic values which will enable recognition to take place. This description is no longer an image, although it can be displayed as an image since the relation of the original pixels to the regions is preserved. This can provide a useful visual check on the process of segmentation.

15.5 Recognition process

The process of recognition requires a knowledge base which describes the characteristics of anatomical regions in a model image. These characteristics are density value, location, size, shape, and other features that may prove useful for recognition. At present these characteristics have been obtained by observation of normal scans and application of anatomical knowledge. The derivation of this knowledge base may well itself be automated in the future by the application of rule formation techniques.

The matching process proceeds sequentially by the use of specialised subroutines to test for each anatomical feature. Tests are made of density, placing, some measure of shape, and adjacency to other anatomical parts already labelled. The segments identified by the segmentation process are by this means given anatomical labels. This four-level structure of pixels, blocks, segments and anatomical regions has been described in further detail[3].

This system has only been tested in a limited manner so far but has shown success already on CT images of the brain. Anatomical structures were labelled correctly and abnormal regions labelled as query regions. The quality of recognition depends on the quality of the segmentation. When segments are too large by being overmerged they were misclassified. When they were too small they remained unclassified. There is clearly need for the ability to correct the segmentation based on partial recognition and feedback. More details and discussion of the whole recognition system can be found elsewhere[4].

15.6   Future programme

This work will now be continuing under the auspices of an Alvey project, entitled 'Model based processing of radiological images' (project number MMI/134). There are seven participating bodies, two of them industrial. It is a three year programme and is designed to yield a system for automatic recognition, with quantitative features, and also for three-dimensional modelling and display of structures, particularly blood vessels.

Our own particular part of the project is concerned with the automatic recognition described above — continuing and refining the work already done. This will involve elaborating the anatomical knowledge base which at present is quite crude and very limited, developing the methods of matching the symbolic description of the image with the anatomical description, improving the process of segmentation, and also using some feedback to re-segment in the light of faulty or questionable recognition, and the development and incorporation of an expert system to control the recognition process. The expertise on expert systems is to be provided by the Turing Institute. General image recognition expertise is to be contributed from Reading University (ex Plymouth Polytechnic) and more particular expertise concerned with other kinds of medical images from Edinburgh University MRC Clinical and Population Cytogenetics Unit. Particular work on modelling of blood vessels already being done will be incorporated and developed by Manchester University Medical Biophysics and St. George's Hospital, London. Industrial involvement is from GEC as the main industrial partner. All participating bodies will be supported by staff and equipment. This is a three-year programme with a carefully detailed plan of tasks and targets.

15.7   Conclusion

The general field of recognition is a topical one. It forms part of the Japanese Fifth Generation initiative and is an important aspect of the British Alvey programme.

Equipment is more suitable now for pursuing it, and languages are available to aid the process. Expert systems are under rapid development and are already used in many different fields. In the field of medical images there has as yet been little use of automatic recognition. Image processing has been extensively used for many years for improving the appearance of images. However structural pattern recognition, which enables the contents of images to be labelled according to anatomy, and irregularities and abnormalities to be recognised automatically, has had little impact so far. The need for it will grow as more complex imaging equipment comes into use requiring more expertise in interpretation. The work we have already done shows its feasibility, and the continuation of it under the auspices of Alvey should lead to clinically useful automatic recognition systems which could be applied to any images in digital form.

References

1   Nagao M and Matsuyama T 1980 *A Structural Analysis of Complex Aerial Photographs* (Plenum Press, New York)
2   Pavlidis T 1980 *Structural Pattern Recognition* (Springer Verlag, Berlin-Heidelberg-New York)
3   Sokolowska E and Newell J A 1986 Multi-layer image representation: structure and application in recognition of parts of brain anatomy *Pattern Recognition Letters* **4** 223–230.
4   Newell J A and Sokolowska E 1986 Model based recognition of CT scan images *MEDINFO86, Proceedings of 5th International Conference on Medical Informatics* (North Holland, Amsterdam)

CHAPTER 16

A Microcomputer Based System for Measuring Regional Heart Muscle Contraction

P F Wankling, R A Perry, J A Newell and M F Shiu
Department of Medical Physics and University Department of Cardiovascular Medicine, Queen Elizabeth Hospital, Birmingham

16.1 Introduction

Cineangiography is well established as a means of imaging the chambers of the heart and the coronary blood vessels as radiopaque contrast is introduced. The film can be used to assess the efficiency of the heart, and various quantitative estimates, such as ejection fractions, may be made. Measurement of regional heart muscle activity is however hampered by the absence of fixed points of reference on the epicardial surface. Established methods use the images from left ventricular filling studies. A series of X-ray images of the left ventricle are obtained as it contracts, by the introduction of radiopaque contrast. The ventricle is divided into sectors and measurements are made or scores assigned to each sector. Various methods for doing this, based on different geometries, have been proposed[1-3]. However since no reference points are used on the epicardial or endocardial surface, any abnormal contractions cannot be attributed to any particular segment of muscle, as they cannot be matched on subsequent frames in the study. Furthermore, the absence of any fixed reference point introduces problems when making measurements of ventricular wall motion relative to the whole heart. Radiopaque markers may be attached to the heart surface and used as reference points[4]. However a surgical operation for this procedure alone is not justified.

An alternative technique for measuring regional muscle activity has been proposed[5], in which coronary artery branching points, imaged during biplanar selective coronary cinearteriography, are used as reference points on the heart surface (*figure 16.1*). Radiopaque contrast is introduced to the coronary arteries via a catheter, and a series of X-ray images of the coronary arteries are obtained. The relative distances between adjacent branching points can be compared for consecutive frames in the study and used as a measure of muscle activity. We have applied this technique to single plane selective coronary cinearteriography and have developed a clinically applicable analysis system based on a microcomputer to measure regional cardiac muscle activity.

The results obtained have been compared with those from conventional analyses of left ventricular wall motion studies. Single plane cineangiograms have been used, taken in the right anterior oblique 30° (RAO 30°) projection. It is recognised that changes in the orientation of the heart as it contracts will lead to an apparent change in the length of an artery segment unless the artery lies in the plane of the film throughout its length. This is approximately true for the left anterior descending artery in the RAO 30° projection as used throughout this study.

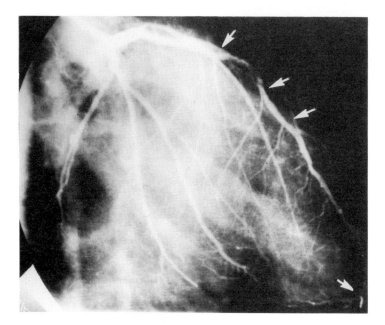

Figure 16.1 A single frame from a cineangiogram showing the left ventricle and left anterior descending coronary artery. Four branching points on the left anterior descending artery are shown by arrows.

16.2 Computer system

An Intertec Data Systems Superbrain microcomputer, utilising programs written in Fortran, is used to process data input via a Summagraphics Bit Pad One digitizer tablet. Routine cineangiograms are projected onto the digitizer tablet and outlines or points are input to the computer.

16.2.1 Ventricular area

The programs written to analyse the left ventricular filling studies facilitate various standard methods. Outlines of the ventricle are entered for the end diastolic frame and the end systolic frame, and the aortic root points (the boundaries between the ventricle and the aorta) are marked on each. The operator must then define a centre point within each outline chosen from one of three options:

1. Centre of mass.
2. Mid-point of the long axis. The long axis is defined as the line between the lowermost aortic root point and the point on the outline furthest away from it (*figure 16.2*).
3. Any point chosen by the operator.

   The outline of the ventricle is divided into up to 50 numbered sectors which each subtend the same angle at the centre point (*figure 16.3*). The sector subtended by the two aortic root points is not included. The area of each sector or the length of a line bisecting each sector may then be calculated. Results from the end diastolic and end systolic frames are then compared and the percentage change relative to a

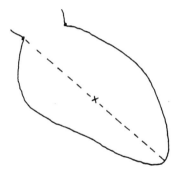

Figure 16.2   Centre of ventricle defined as mid-point of long axis.

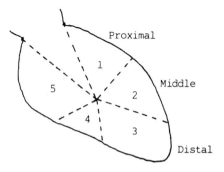

Figure 16.3   Ventricle divided into sectors.

reference frame defined by the operator is displayed. Each step in the analysis is accompanied by appropriate graphics displays to assist the operator.

16.2.2   Coronary artery shortening

Data from cineangiograms showing the left anterior descending coronary artery are input and analysed using separate programs. The outline of the artery from the end diastolic frame is entered into the computer and displayed on the VDU as a guide to subsequent data entry. Artery branching points are then identified and entered into the computer via the digitizer tablet. The projector is then advanced on to the next frame in the study and the same artery branching points are identified and entered into the computer. Each branching point is verified as it is entered and only accepted if it is within a preset distance from a previously entered point and is then assigned to the nearest point. Thus data can be entered in any order and branching points not previously entered are not accepted. As data are entered from subsequent frames their positions are displayed on the VDU together with the outline from the first frame to help the operator keep track of branching points being used in the study. A maximum of twelve points may be entered from up to twenty frames. If a point is not visible on a particular frame, and cannot therefore be entered, its position is assumed by linear interpolation between its positions in frames either side. Once data from all frames have been entered they are stored under the patient's name on a floppy disk.

87

The data are than analysed using a separate program which reads the appropriate coronary artery position data from floppy disk. The computer program is menu driven providing the operator with various facilities. A diagram of the artery as seen in the first frame used, with the branching points numbered on it, is constantly displayed in the top right hand corner of the computer VDU as a reference for the operator. Artery length is calculated as a percentage relative to the first frame or as a percentage reduction relative to the previous frame. Numerical results can then be displayed on the VDU or output to the printer. Results may also be displayed graphically as a series of plots on one set of axes showing the relative length of each artery segment as the heart contracts. The graphs can also be output to the printer using a screen dumping program. The graph showing percentage length relative to the first (end diastolic) frame is found to be the most useful. A gradual reduction in artery length is seen for a normal heart whereas an abnormal heart shows little or no reduction (*figure 16.4*).

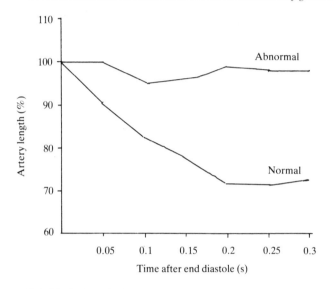

Figure 16.4 Typical results for a single artery segment showing normal and abnormal shortening.

16.3 Comparison of techniques

To examine the effectiveness of the coronary artery shortening technique a comparison was made with the results obtained from conventional analysis of the left ventricular filling studies. The following procedure was used to obtain measurements from cineangiograms taken at 50 frames per second.

For the left ventricular filling studies the mid-point of the long axis was used to define the centre of the ventricle. When the centre of mass was used it was found that errors resulted if the ventricle contracted asymmetrically since the centre of mass shifted towards the segment of the wall which contracted the least and thus falsely increased the apparent contraction[6]. The ventricle was then divided into five segments and the percentage reduction relative to the end diastolic frame was calculated[1].

For the coronary artery shortening studies a series of frames from the study was used beginning with diastole and ending just past systole. The left anterior descending artery was divided into three sections by identifying four branching points. This was typically performed on ten frames at three frame (i.e. 0.06 s) intervals.

The percentage shortening measured in the proximal, middle and distal sections of the coronary artery was then compared with the percentage change in area for the corresponding segments in the ventricular filling studies.

16.4 Results

Thirty eight patients were entered into the trial. Of these nineteen were assessed as having normal heart contraction, and nineteen having abnormal heart contraction, when their left ventricular cineangiograms were examined by two independent observers. The results are shown in *table 16.1*. Significant differences are seen between the normal and abnormal groups in all cases. When the results for the abnormal group were compared good correlation was found between percentage artery shortening and ventricular segment area reduction for total, middle and distal regions, but not for the proximal section. This was attributed to the fact that only three of the abnormal group patients had abnormalities in the proximal region.

Table 16.1   Results of ventricular area and artery shortening measurements on normal and abnormal patients.

1.   Left ventricular area reduction (%)

	Normal mean ± SD	Abnormal mean ± SD
Proximal sector	77 ± 27	57 ± 9
Middle sector	72 ± 27	46 ± 13
Distal sector	63 ± 23	38 ± 9
Total	71 ± 24	48 ± 9

2.   Left anterior descending coronary artery shortening (%)

	Normal mean ± SD	Abnormal mean ± SD
Proximal segment	15 ± 13	5 ± 15
Middle segment	21 ± 10	15 ± 5
Distal segment	18 ± 11	8 ± 9
Total	15 ± 9	9 ± 5

3.   Comparison between two methods for abnormal group

	Correlation coefficient
Proximal section	0.21 (p < 0.2)
Middle section	0.67 (p < 0.001)
Distal section	0.71 (p < 0.001)
Total	0.76 (p < 0.001)

16.5 Conclusions

The artery shortening technique we have described shows good agreement with the established ventricular area technique for the assessment of regional heart wall motion. It has the advantage of fixed reference points on the epicardial surface, enabling segments of muscle to be matched throughout the study and thus improving on the localisation of abnormalities. Many more branching points could be used than described in the above comparison, depending on the quality of the cineangiogram. This would enable a more comprehensive representation of cardiac muscle activity to be obtained.

It is assumed that there is good coupling between artery and cardiac muscle. This has been shown to be a reasonable assumption[5]. Inevitably errors arise in the measurement of artery shortening since we are not using a three dimensional approach. Significant errors may arise at the distal end of the left anterior descending artery as it curls under the apex of the ventricle since the shortest distance between two branching points is measured rather than the arterial path length. Work is in progress to reduce this error. As mentioned in the introduction, errors are introduced if the artery path is not in the plane of the film since there will be an apparent change in artery length as the heart moves. In general this is negligible for the left anterior descending artery imaged in the RAO 30° projection; however errors may be introduced at the distal end of the artery as its direction moves away from the plane of the film.

Computerisation has greatly reduced the time required to process the cineangiogram images when compared with manual methods thus enabling the technique to be used in a routine clinical situation. The hardware required is relatively inexpensive and compact. The software has been written with the untrained operator in mind and very little instruction is required. The calculation time is very small and the results are easily displayed on the VDU or output to a printer as a permanent record. This technique provides a widely applicable method for assessing regional heart wall motion and requires only single plane cineangiograms as the source of data.

References

1 Gelberg H J, Brundage B H, Glantz S and Parmley W W 1979 Quantitative left ventricular wall motion analysis: a comparison of area, chord and radial methods *Circulation* **59** 991–1000
2 Lamberti C, Sanders W J, Yock P and Alderman E L 1984 A system to test methods for ventricular wall motion analysis, in *Computers in cardiology 1984* pp 89–93 (IEEE Computer Society, Salt Lake City, Utah)
3 Lorente P, Azancot I, Masquet C, Duriez M, Babalis D, Nakache J P and Saumont R 1984 Comparison of decision rules in assessing regional wall motion, in *Computers in cardiology 1984* pp 83–88 (IEEE Computer Society, Salt Lake City, Utah)
4 Slager C J, Hooghoudt T E H, Serruys P W, Schuurbiers J C H, Reiber J H C, Meester G T, Verdouw P D and Hugenholtz P G 1986 Quantitative assessment of regional left ventricular motion using endocardial landmarks *J Am Coll Cardiol* **7** 317–326
5 Kong Y, Morris J J and McIntosh H D 1971 Assessment of regional myocardial performance from biplane coronary cineangiograms *The American Journal of Cardiology* **27** 529–537
6 Clayton P D, Jeppson G M and Klausner S C 1982 Should a fixed external reference system be used to analyse left ventricular wall motion? *Circulation* **65** 1518–1521

Discussion on Image Handling

It was stated that the processing power needed for data compression was at present considerable but the necessary alogrithms would shortly be put on to a single microchip and this would perform the data compression and decompression. The performance of the main image processing computer would not then be affected.

The filmless hospital was still thought to be a few years off. This is mainly due to the problems of converting existing X-ray film to a digital format. Present methods of doing this are slow and expensive.

The holographic display system discussed at the meeting should be available commercially in one year and each hologram would cost approximately £6.

The question was raised as to whether pattern recognition worked better on some types of images than others. It was felt that pattern recognition could be applied equally well to all types of images, although the work under discussion had only been applied to CT images. Different techniques would obviously be needed for different types of image. Pattern recognition could also be used to remove image artifacts.

The question was raised as to whether pattern recognition could provide parameters to be entered into a data base to be used by an auto-diagnosis programme. It was felt that this was the next step forward and knowledge bases were already being developed for the interpretation of CT and MRI scans. Pattern recognition could certainly be used to supply data for such a knowledge base.

CHAPTER 17

An Overview of Image Processing in Medicine

A Todd-Pokropek
Department of Medical Physics, University College London

17.1 Introduction

A brief survey of image processing as applied to medical images is given in this chapter. Firstly, a description is given of the form that medical images take, and an indication given of the special problems that arise when they need to be manipulated. Then the use of linear processing as applied to medical images is surveyed, ending with methods of statistical pattern recognition. The use of non-linear methods is discussed, including those of syntactical pattern recognition, artificial intelligence and expert systems.

It is not possible to provide a complete bibliography to accompany this section. The interested reader is recommended to look in the regular image processing literature, for example Rosenfeld and Kak[1]. In the medical field, although there is not as yet a satisfactory overall survey of the field, much information can be found in Barrett and Swindell[2], in Ingram and Block[3], and the series of publications under the general title 'Information Processing in Medical Imaging'[4-6].

17.2 Medical images and their special problems

Most of the conventional image processing techniques have been applied primarily to either satellite images, and/or military images of tanks and rockets. Medical images are significantly different in that the 'target' is rather poorly defined. In an image of a rocket in clouds, the aim of the image processing method is to detect the rocket with the highest probability and to obtain additional information such as orientation etc (usually in as small a time as possible). In a medical image the aim is often to determine in what way the image differs, if at all, from 'normality'. Additional information may also be extracted about the properties of an 'abnormal region', for example its average magnetic resonance (MR) relaxation time etc.

A major aim of all image processing methods is to segment an image, that is, to divide it into regions which have common properties, for example corn-field, forest, river, airport, etc. In medical images, we may attempt to segment an image into bone, soft tissue, lesions, etc. However, the categories into which classification is attempted in medical images are by no means distinct, nor do we have in any way a closed system in which the number of categories are all known and defined.

Finally, many medical images are of relatively low image quality, e.g. the signal to noise ratio is poor. Whereas in many other image processing areas the signal to noise ratio can be improved by observing for longer times, or by increasing the 'intensity' (for example of the source of radiation), this is often not possible in medical images, either from ethical considerations, or simply from the fact that since patients tend to move, increasing the observation time may in fact degrade rather than enhance the image. Most image processing methods work best with high quality images.

17.3 Linear image processing

17.3.1 Deconvolution and variations

All processing implicitly or explicitly is based on a model. The simplest model, often used, is that the imaging system is linear and that the observations **O** (in detector space) depend on the source image **I** (in imaged space), by means of a set of coefficients **A** defined such that

$$O(i,j,..) = \underset{n\,m\,...}{\Sigma\,\Sigma\,..\Sigma}\ A(n,m,....;i,j....)\ I(n,m,...) \qquad (1)$$

A, O and **I** are all multidimensional (for example, the directions x,y,z and time t), and the summation is carried out over all dimensions. **O** and **I** can be simplified by being expressed as one dimensional vectors, by reading out the multidimensional **O**(i,j,...) and **I**(i,j,...) one row (or column) at a time. For example, for a two dimensional N × M set of observations **O**(i,j), we generate the vector

$$O[(0,0),(0,1)...(0,N\text{-}1),(1,0),(1,1),....(1,N\text{-}1)......(M\text{-}1,N\text{-}1)]$$

and correspondingly for **I**

$$I[(0,0),(0,1)...(O,N\text{-}1),(1,0),(1,1),....(1,N\text{-}1)......(M\text{-}1,N\text{-}1)]$$

In this case

$$O(k) = \underset{l}{\Sigma}\ A(k,l)\ I(l) \qquad (2)$$

where the **O** and **I** are vectors indexed by k and l, such that

$$\mathbf{O} = \mathbf{A}\,\mathbf{I} \qquad (3)$$

Such a system is linear (but not necessarily stationary). Many systems are in fact also stationary or may be treated as such. A stationary system may be considered as one where the coefficients A(k,l) do not depend arbitrarily on l (the position in the imaged space) but on l-k, the position of a point in the detected space relative to a point in the imaged space. This means that **A** repeats itself in a circulant manner (it is Toeplitz), such that each row of **A** is identical to the previous row, shifted by one place. Such a matrix can be decomposed into a diagonal matrix by means of the Fourier transform. The model of the system is now that of some kind of convolution,

$$g(x,y) = \underset{x'y'}{\Sigma\,\Sigma}\ h(x\text{-}x',y\text{-}y')\ f(x'y') \qquad (4)$$

$$\text{or} \qquad g(x,y) = h(x,y) * f(x,y) \qquad (5)$$

where g(x,y) is the observed image, f(x,y) is the source image (corresponding to **O** and **I** in the matrix representation), h is the transfer function of the system, and x and y are positions in a cartesian coordinate system.

Thus, a common image processing goal is to find **I** by use of the inverse of **A** since

$$I = A^{-1} O \tag{6}$$

Such a problem is called an inverse problem. It must be stressed that A^{-1} may not exist, or may be very difficult to compute. A standard method for investigating the nature of A^{-1} is to look at its spectrum of singular values. If it has many singular values[7] which are very small, the inverse problem may not be solvable. However, for inverse problems which are well behaved, one method for solving them, given that the forward equation is a convolution such that $g = h*f$, is by means of some kind of deconvolution. For example let the Fourier transform $\mathbf{F}\{\,\}$ of a discrete observed image $g(x,y)$ be given such that

$$G(u,v) = \mathbf{F}\left\{g(x,y)\right\}$$

where

$$G(u,v) = \Sigma \Sigma \, g(x,y) \exp(-i(ux+vy)) \tag{7}$$
$$\quad\quad x \ \ y$$

then by the convolution theorem,

$$\mathbf{F}\left\{g(x,y)\right\} = \mathbf{F}\left\{h(x,y)\right\} \, \mathbf{F}\left\{f(x,y)\right\}$$

and

$$G(u,v) = H(u,v) \, F(u,v) \tag{8}$$

which is a simple pointwise multiplication. The capital letters represent the result of the Fourier transform going from space x,y to frequencies u,v.

Hence

$$f(x,y) = \mathbf{F}^{-1}\left\{G(u,v)/H(u,v)\right\} \tag{9}$$

where $\mathbf{F}^{-1}\{\,\}$ is the inverse Fourier transform. This inverse filtering operation is unsatisfactory since $H(u,v)$ tends to become small or zero as u,v increase. Hence a window function $W(u,v)$ is normally employed such that the estimate of the reconstructed image intensity $f(x,y)$ is given by

$$f(x,y) = \mathbf{F}^{-1}\left\{G(u,v) \, W'(u,v)\right\}$$

$$W'(u,v) = W(u,v)/H(u,v), \quad |H(u,v)| \geq \epsilon$$
$$\quad\quad\quad = 0 \quad\quad\quad\quad\quad\quad |H(u,v)| < \epsilon \tag{10}$$

where ϵ is a small constant.

This operation is essentially one form of a constrained deconvolution. Many variations exist in the choice of window function to be used, see for example references 1,7.

The problem may be looked at more generally. The result of any process such as deconvolution is to produce an estimate $\hat{\mathbf{I}}$ of **I**. However since $\hat{\mathbf{I}}$ is not identical to **I**, then there will be some measure of distance between them which one would normally attempt to minimise, for example the L2 norm D

$$D = \|\hat{\mathbf{I}} - \mathbf{I}\|^2 \qquad (11)$$

which is just the (Euclidean) sum of the squared differences. However, instead, one could minimise

$$\|\hat{\mathbf{I}} - \mathbf{I}\|^2 + \alpha \|\hat{\mathbf{I}}\|^2 \qquad (12)$$

which corresponds to a regularized solution[8,9], for which there is a corresponding window function when expressed in the Fourier domain. In this case, not only does one attempt to obtain a solution which is close to the true solution, but an additional constraint is used in that one looks for that solution which is smoothest and which is close to the true solution. This constraint is controlled by the choice of the weighting parameter α. Among other related techniques are those of Maximum Entropy/Likelihood and Conjugate Gradient methods[10,11].

Tomographic reconstruction is a sub-category of this type of linear processing, where the forward operation, that of observing projections of some object, is represented by the Radon transform, and the inverse operation is (naturally) the Inverse Radon transform, which may be performed via Fourier, regularized, or other techniques. The reader is recommended the book by Natterer[8] for further details.

17.3.2 Matched filtering

The aim of the operations described in the previous section is to recover the original image after it has been modified by some known operation (such as in tomography). Suppose a different aim is required, namely that of extracting a 'signal' from some clutter of information which could be called 'noise', such as detecting a 'tumour' in a CT image. Suppose that the form of the signal (which is spatially invariant) can be described by $s(x,y)$. The underlying model is then

$$g(x,y) = f(x,y) + \mu\, s(x\text{-}x', y\text{-}y') \qquad (13)$$

and in reality the problem reduces to estimating the constants μ, x' and y'; that is how much of the signal is present, and where. The solution to this (rather simplified) problem is by use of the matched filter, that is convolving $g(x,y)$ with $s(-x,-y)$ in the case of white noise. However, the model just described supposed that the whole of the image, other than the signal sought, could be treated as noise, and is therefore almost certainly not white (having constant power with respect to frequency).

In brief, using matrix notation, let $\mathbf{m}$ be a vector generating $\mathbf{f_m}$ from an image $\mathbf{f}'$, being the sum of a signal $\mathbf{f}$ and noise $\mathbf{n}$, where $\mathbf{f_m}$ is the desired filtered image and $\mathbf{m}$ the matched filter for which we are looking. The signal after filtering is $\mathbf{m^T f}$ and the noise power is the expected value of $(\mathbf{m^T n})(\mathbf{m^T n})^T$ which equals $\mathbf{m^T K_n m}$, where the superscript T indicates the transpose, and $\mathbf{K_n}$ is the noise covariance $(\mathbf{nn^T})$. Thus the signal to noise ratio S/N after filtering is equal to

$$S/N = \mathbf{m^T f} / \mathbf{m^T K_n m} \qquad (14)$$

If the signal to noise is to be maximized, then the differential of the signal to noise ratio with respect to $\mathbf{m}$ should be zero, which results[12] in a solution

$$\mathbf{f_m} = \mathbf{f^T K_n^{-1} f'} \qquad (15)$$

where $\mathbf{f}'$ is as defined above

Thus the matched filter in this case is, as before, just a vector correlation with the expected signal, but now after the observed image has been whitened by the inverse of the 'noise' power spectrum. Note that there are still very important assumptions of linearity, stationarity and independence of signal and noise. The image $f_m(x,y)$ created can be thought of as the image of the probability of finding a signal f at each position x,y.

17.3.3 Segementation

The segmentation problem usually consists of indicating, for each point in the image, to which of several classes it belongs. Often, lines are then drawn on the image around clusters of points belonging to the same class. One segmentation method would be to generate a set of matched filtered images, and then to classify each point in the image as belonging to the class corresponding to that matched filtered image with the maximum value at that point. Matched filtering is a global operation, as is deconvolution, where all points in the image are treated identically. The classification operation as just stated is a local operation and is neither linear nor stationary.

The most common segmentation method used is based on edge detection. Here the model assumed supposes that the image is formed of regions where points have similar properties (for example pixel values) and where there is a sharp change from region to region. Thus the difference in value between two points, $g(x_1,y_1)-g(x_2,y_2)$, belonging to the same region is supposed to be much less than if the two points belong to different regions. If this test is performed for adjacent points (in a discrete image) then one is testing $g(x,y)-g(x+1,y)$ and the difference between the other corresponding adjacent points e.g. $g(x,y)-g(x,y+1)$. These values (when normalized) correspond simply to the differential of the image. An edge may be stated to have been detected when this difference is greater than some threshold. Thus let $\delta\{\ \}$ be an operation used to differentiate an image, for example a convolution with a filter of basic form $[1,-1]$, then edge detection is often represented as the operation of finding a matrix of values $E(x,y)$ where each point is either a 1, indicating that an edge is present or else 0, such that

$$E(x,y) = 1 \quad \text{if } \delta\{g(x,y)\} \geq \beta \qquad (16)$$
$$= 0 \quad \text{if } \delta\{g(x,y)\} < \beta$$

where β is some threshold which may be defined locally or globally. A suitable local definition might be based on the local signal to noise ratio in the original image.

The image E consists of just a series of disconnected points indicating that an edge might be present there. These need to be connected together to isolate regions. Additional information such as the possible orientation of the edge (by comparing the partial differential coefficients in x and y) is often helpful. Likewise, the use of an additional window function to improve the signal to noise ratio is often employed. However, the considerable (over)simplicity of the underlying model must be stressed, since the only property used was that points belonging to the same region have values that are close to each other.

An additional constraint may be employed to improve the segmentation, namely that points within a region form a cluster in space, that is, they are adjacent to each other. Additional constraints on contiguity can also be used. Various algorithms such as Split-Merge, Pyramids and region growing are then helpful[13,14]. The basic Split-Merge algorithm may be stated as follows.

1. Form a tree, for example a quad-tree where each of four adjacent (child) pixels in some level n-1 are combined together to form a (parent) node in level n, for example by using a rule such that

$$P_n(i,j) = \sum_{r=0}^{1} \sum_{s=0}^{1} P_{n-1}(2i+r,2j+s) \tag{17}$$

where P_n is the collection of pixel values at some level n. The size of P_n will be ¼ the size of P_{n-1}. P_0 is just the original image g.

2. For all points in the tree $P_n(i,j)$ consider the four pixels in the level n-1 linked to the point i,j in level n. If they are (according to some criterion) nonuniform, the $P_n(i,j)$ is said to be split, and the four linked children treated separately. If, on the other hand, four child components are found to be uniform, they are merged and only the parent is considered.

3. This operation continues until no further splits or merges are possible. Dependent on the criterion used for uniformity, the image can effectively be segmented into regions.

The algorithm can be improved by using a better tree representation, and using iterative approaches. The simple associating rule given above can be replaced also by non-linear or other complex generating rules.

17.3.4 Statistical pattern recognition

Images can be manipulated, for example segmented, based on statistical properties. In the previous section, the use of the expected value of a pixel was used as a classifier. This can be generalized. Given an image with known objects which have been classified, for example different organs and tissue types, then a classifier can be designed which has the optimal linear discriminating properties for those sampled types.

1. Covariance matrix. Many classification techniques use the covariance matrix of the image or the image sample. Given an image **g**, then the correlation matrix **R** is given by

$$\mathbf{R} = E\{\mathbf{g}\,\mathbf{g}^{*T}\} \tag{18}$$

where * indicates the complex conjugate, T the transpose, and $E\{\ \}$ is the expected value. Let **M** be the mean matrix such that m(x,y) is the expected value of g(x,y). The covariance matrix **C** can be found from **R** and **M** from

$$\mathbf{C} = \mathbf{R} - \mathbf{M}\,\mathbf{M}^{*T} \tag{19}$$

The covariance image occurs in many places in image processing, for example in the Karhunen-Loeve (KL) transform.

2. Karhunen-Loeve (KL) transform.[1,7] One definition of the KL transform is from the pairs of equations

$$\mathbf{g}' = \mathbf{A}\,\mathbf{g}$$

$$\text{such that} \quad \mathbf{A}\,\mathbf{C} = \Gamma\,\mathbf{A}. \tag{20}$$

The KL transform is the multiplication of a matrix **A** by **g** to give the transformed matrix $\mathbf{g}'$, such that $\mathbf{C}$, the covariance matrix of $\mathbf{g}$ is 'decomposed' into Γ a diagonal matrix ($\Gamma(i,j)=0$ for $i \neq j$). This transform has the interesting property that it decorrelates the image into a series of basis functions $\mathbf{A}(i)$ and associated weights $\Gamma(i)$ in an 'optimal' fashion, that is the basis functions (rather like the sines and cosines of a Fourier series) are orthogonal, and minimise covariance. It must be pointed out, however, that computing $\mathbf{A}$ and hence Γ is by no means trivial, since if $\mathbf{g}$ is of size n × n then $\mathbf{C}$ is of size n^2 × n^2. Essentially, the image $\mathbf{g}$ can be considered as decomposed into n^2 eigenvectors (or orthogonal images) and n^2 associated weights. Thus in a similar manner to filtering in the Fourier domain, images can be filtered in the KL domain, that is, each component of Γ multiplied by a weight (or window function) before the inverse operation is applied. If this weight is either zero or one, then this is equivalent to retaining certain eigenimages, and discarding the rest, normally those associated with small eigenvalues $\Gamma(i,i)$ and hence presumably containing little signal.

3. Factor analysis. Factor analysis and discriminate function analysis are mathematically quite closely related to the KL transform, many differences being merely questions of normalization. Factor analysis is normally used to study a sequence of images $g(x,y,t)$ where the third dimension is typically, but not necessarily time. In this case, the data set is decomposed into a series of orthogonal eigenvectors, and associated eigenvalues. The orthogonal eigenvectors can be either functions of t, for example $e_k(t)$ and their associated sets of weights $i_k(x,y)$ where the index k refers to the order of the eigenvector, where normally only a few solutions, for example k<4, are retained. Alternatively, a set of eigenimages $i_k(x,y)$ may be generated, together with their associated weights $e_k(t)$.

Such decompositions of images and sequences of images have only statistical significance. They do not as such correspond to any underlying properties of the image, for example, anatomical or physiological functions. For this reason much effort has been expended in attempting to rotate such solutions, forming linear combinations of eigenvectors, which do match desired properties, and retaining the powerful statistical descrimination properties of the original transform. The constraint typically used to determine the rotation is that the solutions should be positive after rotation, as is the case with many physiological functions, but not with the original unrotated solutions.

17.4 Non-linear processing

Linear image processing methods have well-defined limits. For example, no linear filter (which can be represented in the Fourier domain) can change the signal to noise ratio (SNR) at any given spatial frequency. They can change the overall SNR in the image, but only by relying on the fact that the spatial frequency distribution of the signal and the noise (or rather of their power spectra) are different. In order to circumnavigate such limitations, non-linear methods are often employed. A drawback of such methods is often that they cannot be analyzed in the same manner as linear methods. Comparing SNR before and after a non-linear transform (for example when replacing each pixel by its square root) can give misleading results.

A commonly employed non-linear process is that of homomorphic filtering, which, it is suggested, may result in improved 'noise reduction' in comparison to linear filtering operations. Here each pixel $f(x,y)$ is replaced by $\log(f(x,y))$, a filter applied, and the resulting g(x,y) replaced by exp(g(x,y)). This idea is related to that of cepstrum analysis[15]. The complex cepstrum f(n) of some data sequence is given by

$$f(n) = \frac{1}{2\pi i} \int_c \log(F(z)) \, z^{n-1} \, dz \qquad (21)$$

where $F(z)$ is the z Transform of the data sequence, and the integration is normally performed on the circle $z=\exp(\alpha)$, where α, z, F, and the log operation are complex. Cepstrum analysis has been used in many areas, for example deconvolution and texture analysis.

A simpler technique, often helpful, is that of median smoothing. In general, in some region R, the sample estimates are ranked in order and the median determined. This new value may be substituted back at the centre of the region, or some other operation such as estimating the difference between the median and the central value performed. Since the ranking operation is independent of amplitude (it is non-parametric), such operations are often used when large unwanted excursions can be found in the data which need to be eliminated, but without perturbing surrounding values as would occur with any linear filtering process.

Other non-linear processes are often employed in order to exploit the non-stationary nature of the image. Since estimates of signal and noise power spectra can be obtained as a function of position in the image, then non-stationary equivalents of linear filtering operations can be employed, matched to local conditions rather than global values for the whole image. Variable (region dependent) histogram equalization is an example of such a method. Kalman filters[16] are another class of filters with wide applicability to medical images, where a local estimate of the statistical properties of the image can be exploited.

17.5 Preprocessing

The availability of image processing methods as part of the acquisition stage of instrumentation in general, and medical instrumentation in particular, has been revolutionary. In most instruments, problems exist with respect to linearity and stationarity. For example in a CT scanner, the signal observed at some point needs to be normalized with respect to some reference signal. This is often not a linear process (e.g. multiplication by a constant) but is often performed via a look-up table taking into account various sources of error. Likewise spatial distortion is a general problem and can be corrected by taking into account mapping functions relating 'true' positions with observed positions. Similarly, the problem can be attacked in a more general sense by performing a parameter estimation, that is, knowing a set of values related to some observation, deriving a maximum likelihood value for determining the desired output values. As an illustration, in a gamma camera, one might observe a set of signals from a range of photo-multipliers, from which one can derive a maximum likelihood estimate of the position and energy of the interaction of some incident photon with the detector. Many methods used in this area are, however, rather ad hoc in nature, and almost all methods are highly non-linear and non-stationary. A second example is in Digital Subtraction Angiography. Warping is needed to match a (pre-contrast) mask image to an image taken during the passage of contrast, before the two are subtracted.

17.6 Syntactical pattern recognition

Segmentation may be used to determine boundaries around objects, such as organs, tumours, blood vessels etc in radiology, or cells, chromosomes etc in cytological images. Such a boundary is a line which may then be analyzed, as a result of which the object contained within the boundary may be classified. Syntactical pattern recognition methods[17] are often employed for this purpose. The basic concept of such methods is that of a grammar, or set of rules defining relationships between different lexical elements. A lexical element might be simple, (such as a straight line segment in a boundary) or complex (such as 'chromosome type x'). A terminal element is an element that can be observed as such. The grammar is really a set of rules for equivalencing complex elements (such as the latter) into sets of terminal elements (such as the former). These are called 'productions'.

For example, consider a grammar comprising a terminal set Σ of symbols $\{a,b..\}$, a non-terminal set $N = \{A,B..\}$ of symbols which may be considered as variables, a set of productions P being rules relating symbols in Σ and N, and a starting symbol $S \epsilon N$, then a grammar L can be defined as

$$L = (N, \Sigma, P, S) \qquad (22)$$

where for example the production rules might be $S \rightarrow aS, S \rightarrow b$. Given these production rules we can generate strings of form

$$S \rightarrow aS \rightarrow aaS \rightarrow aaaS \rightarrow aaaaS \rightarrow aaaab \qquad (23)$$

Several different types of grammar can be distinguished, essentially those that are context-free (independent), and those that are context-sensitive. For example a 'notch' could be defined at the sequence 'straight line segment' 'acute angle' 'straight line segment', independent of context, whereas 'carotid bifurcation' is much more sensitive to context. The methods of syntactical pattern recognition are in many cases rather like those of list processing as used in LISP and PROLOG. The distinction between being context-free or -sensitive is determined by the possibility of performing some substitution in such a list of elements which is dependent or not on the nature of the adjacent elements. Other types of grammars exist; these are called unrestricted and regular. All regular grammars are context-free, all context-free grammars are context-sensitive (i.e. contained within the set of such grammars) and all context-sensitive grammars are unrestricted (where no constraints on production rules are imposed).

Such methods are of value in classifying structures in cytology, and in the analysis of networks of blood vessels; they have been employed on other types of medical images but the nature of the biological variability of the structures has proved to be a limitation.

17.7 Expert systems and knowledge representation

Syntactical pattern recognition methods may be employed directly in an expert system to interpret images. However, such (brute force) approaches have not proved very successful as yet since it is very hard to define for medical images in general either the appropriate set of 'symbols' or the relevant production rules. Hybrid systems have been employed, using trained observers to extract features, and then, using a learning system and the same observers, to define relationships between these features, which of course include clinical or disease status.

100

Such approaches have been most successful when used to tackle 'annex' problems, for example being used as an 'expert advisor' when looking for features, or pattern matching as employed in computer aided atlases. Here, an atlas of images, for example CT or PET brain slices, has been created. The requirement is to take the clinical image containing unknown features, and to superimpose the appropriate image from the atlas. The atlas image is normally a reduced representation, for example a series of boundary lines in a segmented representation, which may then be distorted or perturbed relatively simply. A set of rules may be defined (often being the topology of the image) to constrain this process. Thus a rule based expert system can be an aid to the superimposition of such images, following which interpretation of the image may be attempted. Another application for such methods is that of tissue typing from MRI data, where again rules can be defined constraining the properties (relaxation times, position, shape etc) of tissue types, as an aid to segmentation.

17.8 Summary

While image processing in medicine uses techniques most of which were developed in other areas, it has special problems and requirements. The lack of ability to define 'signal' in a very precise manner results in images with effectively (and often practically) very poor signal to noise ratios. However, techniques now exist and are widely used for pre-processing data (to eliminate or correct for acquisition distortions), for attacking many inverse problems associated with reconstruction, and for post-processing images to assist with their interpretation. The power of these methods may well lead to a general preference for the use of digital images over their corresponding analogue equivalents, with considerable implications for diagnostic methods in general in medicine.

References

1   Rosenfeld A and Kak A C 1982 *Digital Picture Processing* Vols 1 & 2 (Academic Press, New York)
2   Barrett H H and Swindell W 1981 *Radiological imaging* Vols 1 & 2 (Academic Press, New York)
3   Ingram D and Block R 1985–6 *Mathematical Methods in Medicine* Vols 1 & 2 (John Wiley, Chichester)
4   Di Paola R and Kuhn E, eds 1980 *Information Processing in Medical Imaging* (INSERM, Paris)
5   Deconinck F, ed 1984 *Information Processing in Medical Imaging* (Martinus Nijhoff, Dordrecht)
6   Bacharach S, ed 1986 *Information Processing in Medical Imaging* (Martinus Nijhoff, Dordrecht)
7   Pratt W K 1978 *Digital Image Processing* (John Wiley, New York)
8   Natterer F 1986 *The Mathematics of computerized tomography* (John Wiley, Teubner)
9   Tikhonov A N and Arsenin V Y 1977 *Solutions to ill-posed problems* (Winston, Washington DC)
10 Shepp L A and Vardi Y 1982 Maximum likelihood reconstruction for emission tomography *IEEE Trans Med Imaging* **MI-1** 113–122
11 Huesman R H, Gullberg G T, Greenberg W L and Budinger T F 1977 *Users Manual: Donner Algorithms for reconstruction tomography*. Lawrence Berkeley Lab Pub 214
12 Papoulis A 1968 *Systems and tranforms with applications in Optics* pp 179–193 (McGraw-Hill, New York)
13 Burt P J 1984 The pyramid as a structure for efficient computation, in *Multiresolution image processing and analysis* (ed A Rosenfeld) pp 6–37 (Springer-Verlag, Berlin)

14   Pavlidis T 1982 *Algorithms for graphics and image processing* pp 113–116 (Springer-Verlag, Berlin)
15   Oppenheim A V, Shafer R W and Stockham T G 1968 Nonlinear filtering of multiplied and convolved signals *Proc IEEE* **56** 1264–1292
16   Bozic S M 1979 *Digital and Kalman Filtering* (Edward Arnold, London)
17   Gonzales R C and Thomason M G 1978 *Syntactic pattern recognition: an introduction* (Addison-Wesley, Reading)

Contributors

Dr H Beedie PhD
: Microcomputing officer
Department of Computing
University of Wales Institute of
    Science and Technology
King Edward VII Avenue
Cardiff CF1 3NU

Dr R E Bentley PhD
: Lecturer
Physics Department
Institute of Cancer Research
Downs Road
Sutton
Surrey SM2 5PT

Dr J A Brace PhD
CPhys MInstP
: Top Grade Physicist
Medical Physics Department
The Royal Free Hospital
London NW3 2QG

Dr A J Britten PhD
: Senior Physicist
Wessex Regional Department of Medical Physics
Southampton General Hospital
Southampton SO9 4XY

Mr D McG Clarkson
MPhil
: Senior Physicist
Department of Medical Physics and Bioengineering
Glan Clwyd Hospital
Bodelwyddan
Clwyd LL18 5UJ

Mr A P Davies
: Network Manager
Physics Department
Institute of Cancer Research
Downs Road
Sutton
Surrey SM2 5PT

Mr A R Davies MSc
: Senior Physicist
Department of Medical Physics
Princess Margaret Hospital
Okus Road
Swindon SN1 4JU

Dr John Drinkwater PhD
: Research Assistant
Blackett Laboratory
Imperial College
London SW7 2BZ

Dr J S Fleming PhD
: Principal Physicist
Medical Physics Department
Southampton General Hospital
Southampton SO9 4XY

Mr M Gibson

Medical Laboratory Scientific Officer
Department of Haematology
Glan Clwyd Hospital
Bodelwyddan
Clwyd LL18 5UJ

Mr Stephen Hart

Research Assistant
Blackett Laboratory
Imperial College
London SW7 2BZ

Dr P J Howlett PhD
CEng MIEE

Top Grade Physicist
Wessex Regional Medical Physics Department
St Mary's Hospital
Portsmouth PO3 6AD

Dr P C Jackson PhD
MInstP CPhys

Principal Physicist
Department of Medical Physics
Bristol General Hospital
Guinea Street
Bristol BS1 6SY

Dr D Jennings PhD

Head of Communications Group
Department of Computing
University of Wales Institute of
    Science and Technology
King Edward VII Avenue
Cardiff CF1 3NU

Mr A C Keen

Basic Grade Physicist
Nuclear Medicine Department
Southampton General Hospital
Southampton SO9 4XY

Mr H Key MSc

Basic Grade Physicist
Department of Medical Physics
Bristol General Hospital
Guinea Street
Bristol BS1 6SY

Dr A N R Law MA MSc
PhD

Research Assistant
Department of Biomedical Physics and
    Bioengineering
University of Aberdeen
Foresterhill
Aberdeen AB9 2ZD

Mr C Legg DIC

Applicants Scientist
National Remote Sensing Centre
Royal Aircraft Establishment
Farnborough
Hampshire

Dr J A Newell MA DPhil
CPhys FInstP MBCS

Principal Physicist
Department of Medical Physics and Biomedical
    Engineering
Queen Elizabeth Hospital
Birmingham B15 2TH

Dr R A Perry MRCP

University Department of Cardiovascular Medicine
Queen Elizabeth Hospital
Edgbaston
Birmingham B15 2TH

Ms E M Pitcher MSc

Senior Physicist
Department of Medical Physics
Southmead Hospital
Westbury-on-Trym
Bristol BS10 5NB

Mr D Plummer MA
Dip Comp

Physicist
Department of Medical Phsyics and Bioengineering
University College Hospital
First Floor
Shropshire House
11–20 Capper Street
London WC1E 6JA

Mr Philip G B Ross
MA MSc

Computer Officer
Department of Biomedical Physics and
    Bioengineering
University of Aberdeen
Foresterhill
Aberdeen AB9 2ZD

Mr G S Shentall MSc

Research Fellow
Medical Physics Department
The Royal Free Hospital
London NW3 2QG

Dr M F Shiu FRCP

Senior Lecturer
University Department of Cardiovascular Medicine
Queen Elizabeth Hospital
Edgabston
Birmingham B15 2TH

Dr E Sokolowska PhD

Lecturer
Department of Computer Science
University of Aston
Gosta Green
Birmingham B4 7ET

Mr P H Stevens

Senior Physicist
Department of Medical Physics
Bristol General Hospital
Guinea Street
Bristol BS1 6SY

Dr J Sutcliffe

Lecturer
Department of Medical Physics
The General Infirmary
Leeds LS1 3EX

Mr A Todd-Pokropek
MPhil

Senior Lecturer
Department of Medical Physics
University College
London WC1E 6BT

Mr P Vernon MSc

Physics Manager
IGE Medical Systems Ltd
Colney Street
St Albans
Herts AL2 2ER

Mr P F Wankling MSc

Senior Physicist
Medical Physics Department
Queen Elizabeth Hospital
Edgbaston
Birmingham B15 2TH

Dr S Webb PhD ARCS
DIC

Lecturer
Physics Department
Institute of Cancer Research
Downs Road
Sutton
Surrey SM2 5PT

Mr P Wild

Lecturer
MRC Mineral Metabolism Unit
The General Infirmary
Leeds LS1 3EX

Index